Working for Equality:
policy, politics, people

Richard Freeman, Fiona McHardy
and Danny Murphy (editors)

C|C|W|B press

First published by CCWB Press in 2017
Centre for Confidence and Well-being.
Registered Office Abercorn House,
79 Renfrew Rd, Paisley, PA3 4DA

**A catalogue record of this book is available
from the British Library**
978-0-9933527-5-1

Printed and bound in Great Britain by
Airdrie Print Services.

POSTCARDS FROM SCOTLAND

Series editor: Carol Craig

Advisory group:
Professor Phil Hanlon, Chair,
Centre for Confidence and Well-being;
Fred Shedden

Contents

III Politics

IV People

Foreword

The *Reference Group on In/Equalities* first met in the University of Edinburgh at the end of 2015, and then again every couple of months over the course of 2016. Its members worked (and still work) on inequalities of different kinds in different contexts: including on poverty, employment, education, public health, race, gender and sexuality, and in charities and community organisations, local and national government, in corporations and philanthropic foundations as well as in academic teaching and research.

The idea was to talk. We wanted to share experiences, explore challenges and note successes, develop new, critical and constructive perspectives in the fields in which we worked. To do that we had to leave the silos of our professional and organisational fields, finding a new space in which to engage directly with others we might otherwise never have met – but who, we found, shared remarkably similar problems. In this way, we came to discuss concepts of equality and intersection--ality, regulation and legislation, performance management, electoral and many other kinds of politics, arts and culture, administrative systems and the life stories of individual human beings.

We also had to think differently about just how to talk. This wasn't to be just another meeting, nor a workshop, nor another academic seminar. To give people space meant also giving them time: we met over 24 hours, beginning at the end of an afternoon, picking up again the following morning and working through the whole of the day. Over the course of several meetings, each member of the group contributed what we called a case study – a report from the field describing their work in general terms and then some aspect of it they found difficult or significant, and which they wanted to recognise and reflect upon.

What we talked about is collected here, in this book. We've written up our conversations as postcards, addressed to people we feel we know – to others as concerned about inequalities as we are. They share what we've been doing, why we think it matters, why it's not yet enough. They're meant as interventions in the continuing conversation about inequalities in Scotland, as invitations to pick up these thoughts and ideas and take them somewhere new.

It's in keeping with the spirit of our conversations that contributors should be writing here in a personal capacity rather than on behalf of the organisations for which they work. Some have provided references and further reading, which we've posted to the series website.*

Richard Freeman
Academy of Government
University of Edinburgh
June 2017

---

* http://postcardsfromscotland.co.uk/book12.html

Acknowledgements

We are glad to acknowledge here a number of other scholars and practitioners who contributed to our conversations in various ways, including Katriona Carmichael, Akwugo Emejulu, Rhona Feist, Lily Greenan, Derek Logie, Michael McCarron, Derek McGowan, Andrew Miles, Niamh Moore, Steve Sturdy and Juliet Swann.

The Reference Group was supported by an ESRC Impact Acceleration Account held at the University of Edinburgh. We are grateful to Anne Sofie Laegran, Knowledge Exchange Manager in the College of Arts, Humanities and Social Sciences, for her help and advice at the inception of the project, and to Zain Kurdi, who was its research and communications officer.

Carol Craig has been a challenging yet endlessly encouraging series editor and we remain indebted to her.

Contributors

Ewan Aitken is a former Leader of City of Edinburgh Council, and is now CEO of Cyrenians, a charity supporting people excluded from family, home, work or community

Helen Chambers is co-founder of Inspiring Scotland, a venture philanthropy organisation, and of the Equality Network

Ashlee Christoffersen was a researcher at the Equality Challenge Unit in London and is now a PhD student in Social Policy, University of Edinburgh

Philip Cook is Lecturer in Political Theory in the Department of Politics and International Relations, University of Edinburgh

Richard Freeman is Professor of Social Science and Public Policy, University of Edinburgh

Caroline Gibb is Development Worker for the Equality and Rights Network in Edinburgh

Jatin Haria is Executive Director, Coalition for Racial Equality and Rights

Ann Henderson was Assistant Secretary at the Scottish TUC

Meryl Kenny is Lecturer in Gender and Politics, School of Social and Political Science, University of Edinburgh

Diarmaid Lawlor is Head of Urbanism at Architecture and Design Scotland

Darcy Leigh teaches at the University of Sussex Law School

Jamie Livingstone is Head of Oxfam Scotland

Gerry McCartney is Head of the Scottish Public Health Observatory and Consultant in Public Health at NHS Health Scotland

Rachel McEwen was Senior Special Adviser to Scotland's First Minister 2001-07 and is now Director of Sustainability at energy company SSE plc

Robert McGregor is Community Planning Manager, Fife Council

Fiona McHardy is Research and Information Manager at the Poverty Alliance in Glasgow

Fergus McMillan is Chief Executive of LGBT Youth Scotland

Elinor Mitchell is Deputy Director for Public Bodies and Public Service Reform, Scottish Government

Danny Murphy is a retired Headteacher and Honorary Fellow of the University of Edinburgh

Madelaine Simpkin is an independent social researcher and graduate of the Master of Public Policy Programme, University of Edinburgh

Celine Sinclair is Chief Executive of The Yard, which provides play space for disabled children and young people in the East of Scotland

Katherine Smith is Reader in the Global Public Health Unit, University of Edinburgh

I Equalities

This first section asks what we mean by 'equality'. As we began to talk, we quickly established that equalities are multiple, just as inequalities are.

Philip Cook speaks to a distinction now being drawn by philosophers, which is between distributive and relational equality. The significance of this lies in the claim that it is in our relationships with each other that that we become aware of inequalities, and also through them that those inequalities might be overcome. Danny Murphy then returns to the revolutionary trinity of 'liberty, equality and fraternity', finding new impetus to thought and action in what has been its rather neglected third term, that of fraternity. How might we pursue equality through fraternity? Ashlee Christoffersen picks up the more recent turn among black and feminist activists to the problem and politics of intersectionality. The challenge it raises is to understand and address different dimensions of inequality as they interact with each other in the lives of individuals. Darcy Leigh notes how much equalities work is rightly motivated by an urgent need to act, but points to the importance of also giving due attention to its uncertainties, difficulties and dilemmas.

Together, these contributions mark a theme which became increasingly prominent in our work, as in the rest of this book. How might we think and talk about equalities and inequalities in such a way as to make a difference in the lives of individual human beings?

1. What we talk about when we talk about equality

Philip Cook, University of Edinburgh

Philosophers have different ways of thinking about equality. One of the most important recent contributions is Elizabeth Anderson's idea of relational equality, which recognises the significance of social integration.

WHAT do we talk about when we talk about equality? In our discussions at the Reference Group we talked less about equalising income, and more about building boats; less about equalising opportunities, and more about people chatting together on playground swings; less about equalising outcomes, and more about sharing a communal meal. When we talked about equality, we talked about relationships. When we talked about relationships, we talked about respect. Equalising income, opportunities, and outcomes is important. But a world of equal incomes, opportunities and outcomes in which communities are estranged, in which single mums are stigmatised, and in which vulnerable adults are socially isolated remains unequal.

We heard an inspiring story of bonds of respect forged through a community boat building project. The collaborative work of community boat building fostered solidarity and fraternity. We heard a moving tale of a single mum of two, struggling with poverty and depression, gaining self-esteem through volunteering to help others. Chatting with a community development volunteer while watching her children at a playground, she confided how her confidence had grown through helping others. We heard a powerful narrative about an alcoholic dad who had lost everything, including a relationship with his daughter. Through producing healthy food and sharing meals at a common table with others struggling similarly he stopped drinking, maintained a home, and reconnected with his daughter. He was proud of his contribution to others, and of his stronger relationship with his daughter.

These stories about building boats, chatting in a playground, and sharing a common meal tell us that equality is both a matter of how we distribute society's resources, and of the attitudes we express towards each other. These compelling narratives affirm some important developments in recent political philosophy of social justice.

Equality is a central concern of current thinking about social justice. There is a rich literature that considers such philosophical problems as: *what kind of goods* should we seek to distribute equally? Should we seek to equalise resources that people can use to pursue their goals? Should we seek to equalise the material quality of life, or welfare, that people experience? Beyond this, political philosophers have helped clarify questions regarding *how we should distribute* that which we seek to equalise. Should our goal be that everyone has roughly the same amount of goods? Or should we prioritise giving those who are worst off more? These arguments (and many others connected) are important for anyone with an interest in equality or inequality. They help clarify our thinking to make progress in proposing better answers to the inequalities we face. As important, they improve our defences against those who argue against greater equality. But recent work in the philosophy of social justice has also responded to the kind of intuitions we all recognise when we hear stories such as those above.

We all know that a factory that pays its workers equally, but which disrespects those from an ethnic minority, is unequal. From the point of view of equality, our attitudes towards each other matter as much as the way we distribute society's goods. This concern with the importance of attitudes of respect to equality has become known as 'relational equality' or 'social equality', to distinguish it from questions more concerned with 'distributive equality'. Relational equality trumpets the importance of the attitudes expressed in our social institutions. Our laws around marriage *say something* about how we regard different ways of living in loving relationships. Allowing unreflective racial discrimination in employment practices *says something* about the importance we give to racial equality. Political philosophers working on relational equality have much to offer those seeking a deeper understanding of the significance of relationships to equality.

One of the most important contributions made by a foremost theorist of relational equality, Elizabeth Anderson, emphasises the significance of social integration to greater equality. Segregation, whether along racial, religious, class or other lines, is anathema to social equality. Segregation obstructs relationships, desiccates fraternity, and poisons mutual respect. Sociologists tell us that we have natural tendencies to segregate through clubbing together and excluding others from our familiar groups and their benefits. Social psychologists explain how segregation fuels attitudes of discrimination and stigmatisation towards members of other groups; how we unconsciously think more favourably of those closest to our own groups, and are unfairly suspicious and quick to blame those from other groups for their problems and those of society.

Yearning for segregation is part of the crooked timber of our humanity, but so is aspiring to integration. Such is the natural tendency to club, group, and gang that we need strength to resist it. We need admissions policies that prevent segregation of children at school. We need planning rules that prevent communities living ostracised from each other. We need laws that ensure our workplaces are kaleidoscopic in colour, gender, and ability. We need to be encouraged, persuaded, enticed and incited to integrate. If equality is about distribution of society's goods *and* the quality of our social relationships, we need to guarantee respect for all. We guarantee respect for all through greedily exploiting every opportunity we can muster to build better relationships

When we talked about equality, we talked about relationships. When we talked about relationships we talked about respect. These stories affirmed exciting developments in political philosophy about relational equality. Political philosophers and those working to promote equality have much to offer each other. But I wish everyone who reads this could have heard the talks about building boats, chatting together on playground swings, and sharing in a common meal. These stories were like postcards from a better place, a place that seems utopian to many. But this utopia is real to the boat builders, the confidants on the swings, and those sharing a common table. What can I do, what can you do, to move one step closer to someone more impoverished, or more stigmatised, or more vulnerable than you? What will you talk about when you talk about equality? □

2. Liberty, equality and fraternity in Scotland's schools

Danny Murphy, University of Edinburgh

> Liberty and equality are both desirable, but too much of
> one can lead to too little of the other. Fraternity – the
> value of face-to-face relationships of respect and
> affection – can help establish a fair balance as seen, for
> example, in many school communities.

SCOTLAND'S school education system, particularly its secondary school system, both reflects and contributes to inequalities in a number of inter-related ways. The first and most obvious way is that it is deliberately designed to create and/or measure differences in knowledge and learning capacities through its examination system. Performance in this is then used in high-stakes competitive processes operated by employers, training agencies, colleges and universities, as they select and sort young people for different post-school destinations. Inequality in measured outcome is a design feature of the system.

Secondly the system has very different inputs. Young people who leave school at 18 will have attended school for around 17 per cent of their lives. During the remaining time, the quality of their learning is heavily influenced by their parents and carers, wider family, local environment and the rapidly changing national and global context which they access through personal experience, a variety of traditional curated media, the internet and social media. Abigail McKnight's recent study, 'The Glass Floor', shows how, in the competition for examination success,

19

advantaged parents with high financial, social, networking and/ or occupational capital maximise these differential inputs to ensure that their children do not fail.

A third inequality results from the interests and enthusiasms of the young person which, from the earliest years, are both influenced by their experience of school learning and affect their motivation to learn. The increasingly competitive character of school learning has a particularly strong effect – for some this is positive, encouraging greater efforts to succeed, but demotivation is the result for those who never succeed in the competition, those who are always, in the pejorative language of an earlier school era, at or near the 'bottom of the class'. Young people also make choices based on what they see as both desirable and possible to them in their situation and increasingly assert their right to make such choices as they go through their teenage years. The schooling system, and the broader cultural context of 21st century plural developed societies, encourages, respects and values such choice as an important aspect of democratic living, even where the choices made may lead to undesirable outcomes.

A fourth source of inequality arises from the varied, and potentially intersecting , influences from socio-economic and geographic location, cultural traditions and the related social, cultural and interpretative frames young people use to make sense of their experience.

These different inequalities contribute to and are in their turn influenced by inequalities in examination performance. This is not just about individual capacity or effort – there is a clear relationship between socio-economic background and educational attainment on leaving school in Scotland, as in most developed societies. Although individuals buck the general trend, the statistics for Scotland as a whole show a straight linear relationship between levels of socio-economic advantage and examination performance. This gradient is gentler, however, in Scotland than in most other OECD countries. Scotland also has more resilient students (those from poorer socio-economic backgrounds who do well educationally). It also has more socially inclusive schools – where young people from unequal backgrounds mix in the same comprehensive secondary school – than the OECD average. Nevertheless, there is a gradient in examination attainment and the current government is determined to reduce it, to 'close the gap'.

This may be more easily said than done. Additional money is now going in to support the learning of children from less advantaged backgrounds and this will no doubt be put to good use, and will often improve their educational experiences – a very desirable outcome. There have, indeed, already been significant improvements in the attainment levels of the poorest attaining groups over the past twenty-five to thirty years, but every group, including the highest attaining, has also improved. In a competitive process, the most advantaged do not stand still and wait for others to catch up. They continue to use their competitive advantages to keep ahead.

These issues benefit from being viewed through a wider set of lenses. We need to explore the concept of equality and ask what kind of equality is desirable? In school education, equality of opportunity is much used, but is clearly a weaker form of equality than equality of outcome. Also important, as highlighted above, is equality of input. Equality of value – that each child and young person is respected and valued equally – is often missing from national debates, but is vital within school communities where an important message is 'whatever the inequalities in wider society, every single one of you is equally important to us in here'.

In our recent review of the first fifty years of Scotland's comprehensive secondary school system, I and my colleagues at Edinburgh University considered the desirable 'equalities' of democratic school education in the context of the other important democratic principles of 'liberty' and 'fraternity'. Where individuals or groups are free to choose different paths in work or leisure or politics or lifestyle, there will inevitably be diverse, unequal outcomes. Given the freedom to do so those with advantages of wealth, knowledge and social influence, for example, use their advantages to maintain their position. Liberty and equality are in constant tension, and political leaders have to find a balance that will command support in the country at large. Increases in equality can often only come at the expense of such liberty by, for example, evening out financial advantage to some extent through taxation revenue spent on education for all.

The interaction of liberty and equality is complicated. Over the past fifty years, for example, much larger numbers of young people have stayed in full time education beyond the years of compulsory schooling (at age 19, only 18 per cent were in full-time education in 1977, compared to 63 per cent by 2010) – this could be seen as an increase in 'equality'. However, there are significant 'inequalities' within the tertiary sector: those in further and higher education now bear more of the cost of their education individually, while the site of 'positional advantage' has shifted, for many, to the post-graduate phase, where unfunded Masters degrees or unpaid internships continue to give those with access to private wealth competitive advantages in the labour market.

Another important value for schools, and less commonly heard in contemporary political debate, is what Bernard Crick called the 'forgotten value' of fraternity. Fraternity, stripped of its gendered overtones, is about personal face-to-face relationships. It involves empathy and emotion, relationships of warmth, affiliation and respect. Fraternity is a key purpose as well as a key value of democracy, where people are called to compromise and negotiate, share activities and share spaces, on a basis of mutual tolerance and respect. It is easy to ignore the interests of someone you never have to meet, much harder to do this face-to-face. In school settings 'fraternity', often missing from debates at a national or theoretical level, comes into its own. Many of the day-to-day challenges of school life can be boiled down to arguments about the balance to be struck between liberty and equality in a given situation – whose freedom is to be restricted to ensure greater equality? Fraternity, and its face-to-face recognition of the value of the other, eases the resolution of such potential conflicts of interests or values.

In my role as a headteacher within a school community, I often found that a fourth political principle, equity, also came into play in the daily life of the school: were the inevitable conflicts of interests or values resolved *fairly*? Pupils and parents would often accept a limitation on their freedom or an apparent inequality of input or outcome, if they believed that the process followed was fair, and those making the decisions were trusted. However, the pressures on schools to select and sort young people for different post-school destinations continue to make it difficult for schools to value all equally, when the only public measure of their achievement, the examination system, is clearly designed to do exactly the opposite.

Individuals may not have equal value in the labour market, or as potential tertiary sector students, but they do have equal value in their own right. The democratic principle that every human life has equal value should be reflected more fully at every stage of our school system. I have argued that Scotland should accord *equal value* to young people by developing a broadly based non-competitive graduation certificate, accessible *to all* at age 18 – one that includes examination success, but also the many other desirable attributes, skills and achievements which individual young people can cultivate and develop throughout their time in school education. The process of 'graduation' from school education, capturing equally for each individual their special character and talents, has the potential to balance the selective function of school education for potentially unequal futures with the core educational message that each individual is uniquely precious. □

3. Intersectionality and why it matters

Ashlee Christoffersen, University of Edinburgh

Intersectionality is the idea that inequalities interact. Inequalities of class, race and gender, for example, may all be experienced by a single individual at one and the same time, and their specific combination has specific effects. This challenges us to develop new forms of thought and action.

THERE are many different definitions of intersectionality; the one offered here is the understanding that social divisions, and the social positions that they create, are interconnected, interdependent and indivisible from one another. Social positions are shaped by several, co-constituting, factors or divisions operating at the same time. These factors can be analysed at different levels and include, among others, race, sexuality, gender, deafness, disability status, age, class, nationality, and faith.

The term itself is credited to black feminist and legal scholar Kimberlé Crenshaw, who first published it in 1989, but the idea was used in black women's thought and writing going back much further than this. Though now you may hear intersectionality being referred to as 'academic', its early articulations were in the context of engagement in social movements. Crenshaw employed the term to describe the ways that black women's experiences and identities are marginalised by tendencies to treat race and gender as mutually exclusive categories in antidiscrimination law, feminism, and antiracist

25

movements, with all focusing on the most powerful/privileged members of groups (white women, black men) and taking them as representatives of the group as a whole, using examples of legal cases wherein black women were forced to choose between bringing a claim of discrimination on the basis of either race or gender, and could not say that they had been discriminated against because of both.

Factors or social divisions are inseparable from one another because they constitute one another, so for instance at an individual level a person is not a lesbian on the one hand and disabled on the other; rather they are the combination of these at the same time. These different elements form and inform each other and are not lived or experienced as separate. Intersectionality recognises that at the 'intersection' of two or more social divisions, there is a different status that is more than just the 'sum of its parts'.

An intersectional perspective therefore tells us that social groups are never homogenous, and there is no 'essence' of an aspect of identity/experience that holds true across all its intersections. Within social groups, there will always be similarities and differences in identity and experience at the same time, and equality as a goal is therefore not principled on sameness, but on coalition and solidarity which account for difference and recognise that there can still be common issues and interests.

As theory and practice, intersectionality is fundamentally oriented toward social transformation. The relationship between the concept and its application in practice is still being developed, as intersectionality is increasingly invoked in Scottish equality policy. As the term comes to be more widely used, its meaning becomes increasingly contested and it can be co-opted: it has been observed that among some European writers on intersectionality, for instance, it has deliberately lost a focus on race, which is integral to it.

From an intersectional perspective, it is unhelpful to make comparisons between different 'equality groups', e.g. between 'women' and 'disabled people', or to imagine 'hierarchies' of equality, e.g. between race and sexuality, because when doing so the existence/experiences of disabled women, and Black and Minority Ethnic and Lesbian, Gay and Bisexual people, are marginalised and misrepresented. It can also be unhelpful to think in terms of 'multiple identities', or 'multiple discrimination', as identities and experiences are not really 'multiple'; rather, they are intersectional, formed of different elements at the same time.

Intersectionality advocates argue that a focus on addressing the issues affecting those who are most/multiply disadvantaged is the most effective way to address social justice issues, as by doing this those who are singularly disadvantaged will also gain. Ultimately, it is not possible for one social group to 'have' equality, unless everyone 'has' it, because that social group will be intersected by others.

At a recent event on intersectionality for voluntary sector practitioners, I observed a tendency within the group, after hearing intersectionality described, to think along the lines of, okay, so everyone is both oppressed and privileged at the same time, therefore all facets of identity are relevant and somehow kind of the same and equally important to consider in connection to a given social issue. But I don't think this is what intersectionality theory is telling us. In fact, at specific points of

27

time and place, some social divisions can be more important than others in constructing certain positions and experiences. Working intersectionally, it may still be right to set target communities and to recognise that some elements of identity are more important in a particular context than others; but the target community will also have lots of other points of intersection – will not be mutually exclusive to anything or internally homogenous. In fact, if we are not naming and setting priorities and targets, then we are most often falling into considering the most privileged members of social groups as representing the group as a whole, and therefore back to considering social categories as being mutually exclusive.

It is entirely possible and perhaps even common to use the language of intersectionality to resist intersectionality, and we would do well to be mindful of this in considering our own efforts as well as those of others. 'Intersectionality' can for example be used as a rationale to resist a focus or action on a particular marginalised or under-represented group. It can be taken to mean that all groups need to be addressed, in a generic way, with groups still being thought of as singular or homogenous. In contrast, intersectionality alerts us to difference, while helping us to be mindful of its complexity, in seeking equitable outcomes for diverse groups. ☐

4. Equality, instrumentality, uncertainty

Darcy Leigh, University of Sussex

Taking action against inequalities requires clarity, certainty and strategic, goal-oriented action. But making room for new ideas, voices and people – particularly where inequality is concerned – requires openness, uncertainty and ambiguity too.

ONE of the most striking features of the In/Equalities Reference Group was the persistent uncertainty with which it operated. Nobody knew when they got involved quite what they were getting involved with. Despite initial agenda-setting exercises, participants remained uncertain as to the precise purpose of the group. What was the group supposed to *do?* What was it *for?* When I talked with participants about the group, they returned again and again to this persistent uncertainty – this absence of any clear instrumentality – as definitive of their experience. Some told me that this uncertainty was exciting for them – that they rarely got to experience such free space, to explore ideas, such looseness, or to experiment, in their own high-pressure policy-oriented jobs. Others told me that the uncertainty was frustrating for them – that there was no space in those high-pressure policy-oriented jobs for uncertainty and that uncertainty couldn't be instrumentalised, didn't translate usefully back into their daily outcome-oriented equalities work. Some told me that they felt both excitement and frustration about the persistent uncertainty of the group.

Perhaps some of this will sound familiar to policy and

equalities workers who have worked with academics, and academics who have worked with policy and equalities workers. While academics (like me) tend to 'explore' ideas, critique the taken-for-granted and revel in complexity, those who work with policy directly often accuse us of being 'overly academic', responding with 'yes, that's great, but what do I *do* with that?'

The implication here is that academics are not so great at goals, action and instrumentality. This is probably true. Certainly, one of the limitations of academic thought is that it is not often enough addressed to the question 'what shall we do?' It is also a limit of academic communication that it is often not intelligible enough to the people with whom we're concerned. An idea might be overly academic because academics are invested in maintaining their expert statuses and privilege, or because they simply lack the language to communicate it in some other way.

For policy and equalities workers, on the other hand, suspending certainty comes with risks. For leaders in an equalities sector that faces growing inequality, funding cuts and all the pressures of working in a neoliberal capitalist economy, the risks of suspending instrumentality are material and even existential. The equalities sector is fundamentally instrumental: it has aims, it develops strategies and acts to achieve those aims. A project that involves no central instrumentality sounds absurd in this context. A project that suspends certainty and instrumentality requires us to risk discomfort, not-knowing, lacking authority, fumbling, inefficiency, and even wasting our time – all of which likely generated some of the frustration felt by some participants in the Reference Group.

But what do we lose if we refuse all uncertainty, if we insist on immediate and constant instrumentality? Whose knowledge fails to register in instrumental, goal-oriented terms? If we dismiss an idea as overly academic or overly mundane, overly critical or overly crude, we risk letting our language and our instrumentality silence and exclude certain ideas and people. Perhaps this doesn't matter if those who are excluded are status-seeking middle class academics: these are not generally the people with whom equalities work is concerned. But if those people sometimes bring difficult ideas because their suffering is in part caused or ignored by the logics of instrumentality, performance and accounting, for example, and if those people are already among the most marginalised, then this exclusion is something with which equalities workers should be very greatly concerned. Put simply, our concern with outcomes sometimes risks entrenching inequality rather than challenging it.

Here, there is a case to be made for sitting with uncertainty and non-instrumentality, for risking discomfort, for suspending the urge for certainty. This suspension need not be permanent nor is it appropriate for all contexts. The question 'what shall we do?' clearly remains essential to equalities work. This suspension might be momentary or, as it was in the Reference Group, periodic. However we decide to engage – or suspend – instrumentality, we must be vigilant about its limits. Instrumentality reaches its limits when it excludes the voices and ideas of the very people with whom equalities workers are so concerned. When the logics of goals and outcomes reinforce the very systems we are trying to change, then far from being tools or instruments of equality they (and we) become instruments of inequality. □

II Policy

This section turns to the scope and limits of social and public policy in addressing inequalities. We might understand policy very simply as 'what governments do', though we know that what they do is rarely very simple at all.

Robert McGregor begins by exploring the work of Fairness Commissions, and Rachel McEwen explains how businesses have come to adopt the Living Wage. Katherine Smith goes on to argue that ideas are as important to policy making as evidence is, while Richard Freeman explores why we can't change the world just by changing the rules. Helen Chambers suggests that our standard model of the policy process is no longer fit for purpose. For Madelaine Simpkin and Elinor Mitchell, the challenge is to recognise and develop 'the work of talk' in policy making.

5. Fairness Commissions

Robert McGregor, Fife Council

> If Fairness Commissions are to be a true catalyst for change,
> we need them to deliver inspiring reports, and ensure that
> local leaders are committed to doing things differently.

MANY Fairness Commissions have been established in recent years. The Fairer Fife Commission is an example, and the experience of supporting it has provided the basis for this contribution. Like many others, the Fife Commission was set up to re-invigorate local thinking and achieve a step-change in tackling poverty and reducing inequalities. It was wholly independent of the local authority. Its members came from the public sector, academia, charities and the wider third sector, and business but did not directly include community members. Not untypically, it completed its work within a calendar year.

Key success factors included the leadership of the Commission, the experience and expertise that its members brought, and how they worked as a team. Support to Commissions is critical, particularly in helping them to access local evidence. They must be seen to bring a new knowledge and dynamic, and to genuinely commit to listening to community voices experiencing poverty and inequality. Inviting senior public, private and third sector representatives to take part in the process of the Commission, and challenging them to consider what they could do differently, increases ownership of the Commission's work and can aid the transition from deliberation to delivery.

The task of a Fairness Commission is a tough one: defining their task, filtering local evidence, agreeing key messages, and presenting them in a way that powerfully engages their target audiences. Usually it is the report that is the Commission's legacy. The hard shift to produce a report that hits the spot locally is only the start. Next comes the challenge of turning rhetoric into action – most challenging when the Commission stimulates a new optimism, an expectation that big change is possible.

The 2015 report of the Fairer Fife Commission set high ambitions through stretching targets for 2030. It promoted a focus on the resources available rather than those to be cut, urged local players to develop their ways of working and featured a menu of 40 policy and practice recommendations. Critically, it did not aim to set a blueprint for action, but rather to inspire those with access to local levers of change and to influence those controlling national ones.

For all Commissions the challenge of moving to action has been daunting, and they have had to evolve their thinking on ways and means. Ideally, as in Fife, local leaders should be at the front unequivocally, and loudly, championing the Fairness agenda. Explicit linkage to a national Fairer Scotland agenda adds legitimacy and weight. A strong communications approach designed to engage the many and encourage ownership and responsibility is critical. On the nuts and bolts, there must be a manageable action programme with clear governance and good support arrangements, allied with a coalition of the willing-and-able to drive priorities. It cannot be about doing things the same old way. Instead, there should be a commitment to widening partnerships, putting communities at the heart of planning and delivery, prioritising prevention, introducing localised testing, and empowering staff. Easier wins should be pursued, but also a parallel track to tackle the innovative and inspiring. The Commission's programme should include mechanisms to aid sharing and learning, and to explore synergies.

It is critical that Fairness is not seen as the interest of the few. Fairness needs to sit centre-stage. It needs to impact upon how we plan for inclusive economic growth (the balancing of prosperity and fairness); on how we support people into sustainable, fair jobs; and how we plan children's services, health and social care, and health improvement. Leaders and practitioners need to make day-to-day connections to fairness ambitions.

To dispatch the specific recommendations of the Fairer Fife Commission, we developed an action programme for the first three years. It concentrates on a subset of action areas. Leads have been agreed, tasked with setting milestones and reporting monthly. The group of leads meet regularly as an Action Learning Set. This group promotes discussion on different, more sustainable ways of working.

Throughout the Commission's term we organised regular external communications on our activity and emerging findings. We have continued to use Fairer Fife branding to report intentions and success. We plan to expose our first action plan to wider public scrutiny, and are gathering Fairness pledges from leaders, agencies and businesses. We need to do more to bring attention to other fairness achievements where initiatives cannot be directly attributable to our formal programme but share the Commission's ambition and boldness and promote different ways of working.

So, to date, what successes can be attributed to this more

focused fairness ambition? In Fife, these include: The development of ground-breaking strategic assessments that significantly strengthen our understanding of local needs, what has worked and what has not; the delivery of a first tranche of poverty awareness training for up to 600 front line staff; the development of a burgeoning participatory budgeting programme that devolves decision making to local communities; the establishment of a local social enterprise lender to offer an alternative to high-cost online, retail and doorstep lending; strong first steps to address the 'cost of the school day'; and prominence given to running a Universal Basic Income pilot.

In conclusion, the task of Fairness Commissions in assembling realistic but game-changing messages is a very difficult one, but essential given the challenge of moving to effective actions when what happens in local areas is headed by a slow-moving local authority juggernaut. There are some vexing questions. Does every local area need a Commission? What architecture do we need to share lessons from Commissions' work in real time? Do we need to do more to build a fairness movement? Should we be demanding more of the business sector? What should we expect from communities and what support do they need to play the fullest role?

Likely we will see more Fairness Commissions. This is welcome and important, and we need to build on what we've learned to ensure they work to maximum effect. □

6. The business of a Living Wage

Rachel McEwen, SSE

The Living Wage is calculated to allow people to live a decent life, to do more than just survive, and there are now nearly 1,000 accredited Living Wage employers in Scotland.

THERE is nothing about the idea of fairness to argue with. The pursuit of fairness galvanises politicians across the spectrum and is a concept that resonates even with the smallest children. But it is, of course, an entirely subjective concept. What is fair to one might be unfair to another. There are times, however, when an idea captures the imagination of the majority and its simplicity encapsulates the notion of fairness perfectly. For me, the Living Wage does exactly that.

We now know the majority of people who live in poverty live in a household where someone works. Latest data shows that 70 per cent of children in poverty are in households where someone is in work. In other words, it is a myth that poverty relates to the 'work shy' or the idle. Most people in poverty earn their poverty, they don't claim it. Economic inequality isn't just a lack of money; it is a lack of agency to participate in society. Poverty prevents a parent organising a birthday party for their five-year-old, means a family can't have an evening out at the cinema or an avid football fan can't attend a match. These are activities that make life worthwhile. After all, what is it to be human if we can't be social animals?

The central proposition of the Living Wage is that it is a rate of pay that allows you to live, not just survive. It allows you to have a life free from the oppression of poverty. What's more, it assumes that no matter what job you do you deserve to earn enough to live a decent life.

The Living Wage is not the same as a statutory minimum wage, which considers wider economic influences and the labour market as a whole. The Living Wage is all about the individual, their life and that of their family. For Living Wage employers, they are making a voluntary choice to go above and beyond the statutory minimum. These employers discover many happy consequences too: retention rates increase, employee engagement improves and company reputation benefits.

SSE, a large, UK listed, Scottish headquartered company, found the case made by the Living Wage campaigners highly compelling. How could it be fair some of our employees were earning a rate of pay that meant they were on the breadline?

So in 2013, SSE became the 322nd company to become an accredited Living Wage employer. We were the biggest FTSE company at the time to join the movement, the only energy company and one of the first in Scotland. We increased the pay of 158 employees who were receiving the national minimum wage and we began to implement a 'Living Wage Clause' into our service and works contracts. If SSE employees were to receive a Living Wage, it seemed unfair if contracted workers earned less. We estimate that a further 720 contracted workers received a pay rise in 2016/17 as a result of this policy.

We signed up to the Living Wage because we wanted to. We believed it was the right thing to do but in hindsight it had a profound impact in ways we had not envisaged. We expected those who received a pay rise to be pleased. What we hadn't anticipated was how important this signal on fair pay would be to everyone else in the company. It lifted spirits and improved everyone's morale.

At that time, while there were 322 Living Wage employers in the UK, there were only 8 in Scotland. That represented less than 3 per cent of the UK total – and with a population share of nearly 9 per cent, the concept had simply not taken off in Scotland. So Living Wage campaigners in the north and the south decided something needed to be done. The Scottish Government funded – with a small amount of money – an accreditation officer to help companies meet the Living Wage criteria. A business leadship group was established – which a range of employers including SSE, Standard Life and KPMG – and a cross party consensus was found. By early 2017, every single political party leader in Scotland had committed to being a Living Wage employer. All of that activity meant that Scottish businesses sat up and took notice.

The Living Wage was popular with customers and communities and a warm glow was attached to any company that was LW accredited. The First Minister announced the 50th, 100th, 250th and 500th new employer that became accredited. Today, there is a team of four accreditation officers, working flat out on new accreditations. Scotland has nearly 1,000 accredited employers – and this now represents 28 per cent of the UK total.

In November each year the Living Wage Movement, now comprising almost 3,500 UK employers alongside a deep, interconnected and energetic civil society campaign, promotes the new Living Wage rate for the year ahead and celebrates those employers who have voluntarily signed up. It is a remarkable movement that has, truly, made a difference to the lives of thousands of low paid working people. What could be fairer than that? □

7. Information or ideas?

Katherine Smith, University of Edinburgh

What matters most in combatting inequality? Is it information and evidence, or values and ideas?

ACROSS the UK, but particularly in Scotland, there has been a stated policy desire to reduce health inequalities for nearly two decades. Yet, despite a mass of research and raft of policy initiatives, current indicators suggest either that health inequalities have continued to widen or that progress has been remarkably limited. This failure, which has occurred across the UK, has led to some reflection among researchers working in this field, with two, distinct explanations both attracting much support. For some, it reflects failings in the evidence-base: health inequalities researchers have simply not been able to advise policymakers 'what works' in tackling health inequalities. Others, however, take a much more normative (values-based) view, arguing that the policies put in place to tackle health inequalities were shaped by ideological commitments to national economic growth, limited state intervention in markets and, more recently, a need to reduce the public deficit. In other words, some people think the failure is down to *information* and others to *ideas*.

This difference is important because each leads to different conclusions about the best way forward. If you think the issue is a lack of information, the obvious response is to continue investing in research to explore how various interventions and policy changes impact on health inequalities. If, however, you are more persuaded that ideas and values lie at the core of this policy failure, then you may conclude that success requires political action.

Here, I explain why I'm personally more persuaded that *ideas* are core to understanding the failure to reduce health inequalities. These reflections are informed by research I conducted as part of an interview-based PhD exploring the relationship between health inequalities evidence and policy in Scotland and England (a project prompted by my own experience of the limited credibility attached to academic expertise in Scotland's health policy world). I go on to consider the implications of this argument for folk who (like me) work in jobs that focus on the production of information.

The first, and most obvious point was that everyone I spoke to was talking about ideas: civil servants and politicians told me they saw academics as a potential 'source' of ideas; researchers working in a variety of contexts described working to promote research-informed ideas in large and competitive 'markets'; senior civil servants and policy advisors recounted trying to 'sell' ideas to particular ministers. Everybody, it seemed, was in the business of ideas, including those using evidence to make specific ideas more or less persuasive to others.

Secondly, the civil servants and politicians I interviewed had often encountered the same research (and the same researchers) in health inequalities debates as one another and yet reached different conclusions from each other (and from researchers) about the policy implications of particular studies. It was clear, then, that evidence does not speak for itself.

Thirdly, when people working in policy settings explained how and why they reached particular conclusions about the best way forward on a particular issue, it almost always involved reference to overarching ideas. An explicit example of this was the consistent concern I encountered in policy settings as to how policies to tackle health inequalities could be made to fit with ideas about achieving national economic growth. In other cases, ideas seemed more embedded and taken for granted – ideas, for example, about what 'health policy' involves and the appropriate roles and divisions of work in departments of health. Here, I could see Max Weber's ideas about bureaucracy in action – the health departments/directorates I looked at were organised around a medical model of health which divided people into units focusing on particular parts of the health care system, particular population groups and specific risk factors. This meant that ideas relating to the social determinants of health (i.e. the ways in which the conditions in which we live and work – our education, housing, neighbourhoods, employment, etc – impact on our health) were constantly being 'filtered out' or fractured, despite strong supporting evidence, since, in practical terms, these policy levers were often well beyond the remit of health teams.

And finally, similar processes seemed to occur in research, with academics' personal experiences, disciplinary training, normative positions and career-ambitions combining to inform the questions they asked, the methods they used, the conclusions they reached and the 'messages' they packaged and promoted to policy audiences. While everyone treated the evidence they produced and analysed seriously, they necessarily viewed this through the lens of a range of ideas they held about the topic and the organisational, political and funding contexts in which they were operating.

For anyone who is politically engaged, or who has been trained in political or social science, these conclusions may seem so obvious as to be mundane. And yet, the notion that difficult political problems would be solved if we could only get policy-makers to use the best available evidence seems alive and well. The sociologist Steve Fuller has rather cynically suggested that this idea persists because it suits both politicians looking for a reason not to take action ('commission more research. . .') and researchers looking for future research grant income ('commission me to do more research. . .').

While I think Fuller has a point, I continue to believe that research has the potential to play a valuable role in society – I just don't think evidence alone is the solution to the kinds of complex, ethical social problems that policymakers are so often addressing (such as tackling health and wider social inequalities). Indeed, I find myself agreeing with Weber that the role of science is not to tell us (or our political leaders) what we (or they) should do, or how we should live, but rather to make more meaningful choices possible. For me, in practical terms, this means finding ways to ensure that people are able to meaningfully engage with research evidence. And in a democracy, this shouldn't simply be the people academics often ubiquitously refer to as 'policymakers'. Rather, we need to get much better at creating deliberative spaces in which researchers, policymakers and members of the public come together to discuss and debate evidence in ways that acknowledge the role of values and ideas. □

8. The role of rules

Richard Freeman, University of Edinburgh

> We can do much by changing the law, but changing the law isn't always enough to change the world.

ONE of the Reference Group's early discussions explored the scope and limits of law in promoting equality and addressing inequality. Our conversation was broad and wide-ranging, and covered other kinds of regulation, such as rules, guidelines and reporting requirements. This summary picks up some of the issues we raised.

Law is an effective focus for equalities campaigns: a demand for new legislation, or changes to existing legislation provides a readily identifiable target, a point of orientation and a focus for organisation. That said, changing the law is difficult and takes a long time, and changing the law doesn't immediately change the world. The law is an important instrument of change, a powerful lever but no more than that.

Implementing the law – making the rule a reality – requires resources. It may be that a child with special needs is entitled to a place in a mainstream local school, but without special support she may be unable to take it up. It may be easier to change the law where the resource implications are limited, as in the legalisation of gay marriage, or the prohibition of hate crime.

The law doesn't speak for itself, but must be interpreted and applied in practice, by individuals in interaction with others (if it were always clear what the law meant and how it should be used, we would have no need of lawyers, courts and judges). The interpretation and application of most rules and regulations are made according to the norms and conventions of the relevant community of practitioners, professionals or policy makers. In other words, for changing the law to be really effective, we need to change assumptions about the normal enactment of the law.

Meanwhile, we should be wary of thinking that law changes behaviour in any linear fashion, that legal or regulatory change precedes behavioural change. Often, changing the rules is done to ratify a change in behaviour, to consolidate and make sense of an emerging consensus, expressed in practice, that we should do things differently. In this sense, changed behaviour some-times changes the law.

There are aspects of management that work much like law. We talked about other forms of regulation, such as target-setting and monitoring among a range of ways of producing data for the sake of organisational accountability. Generating and collect-ing data may serve an important end in itself, in that it draws attention to issues which might otherwise be ignored. Counting the number of black and ethnic minority employees in a council, for example, makes us think about whether it's proportionate to the number in the general population – and if it isn't, why that should be and what should be done about it. In this way, targets serve as something against which individuals, voluntary and private sector organisations and public bodies can be held to account for the ways they work and the effects of what they do and don't do.

Yet this conversion of people and practices into numbers, of individual and organisational activity into indicators renders them equivalent but not equal. It exposes them to comparison one with another, for good and ill; comparison leads quickly to competition, which may or may not have an equalising effect. Producing, sorting and reporting data in this way comes at significant organisational cost. There may be an inevitable tension – and necessary balance to be struck – between reporting what we do, identifying what we might do and simply getting on with doing it.

Like rules, data need to be talked about. A statistic often makes a good headline, but needs to be interrogated, too: we need always to ask what the numbers really mean, to take account of the complex nature of the reality they seem to represent.

The work of monitoring, meanwhile, like the work of legislation, seems never to be complete. Questions raised by performance data seem to require yet more data to answer them. New laws may achieve much, but invariably have the effect of laying bare what more needs to be done. Standards achieved and targets met invite the setting of newer, higher targets and standards.

Throughout our discussion, there was a sense of the fundamental importance of different forms of law and regulation, but a degree of ambivalence, too. Almost all of us have advocated legal and regulatory change of one kind or another, have been involved in writing rules and guidelines, are engaged in the continual production and distribution of data, yet we are profoundly aware of the limits of what they can achieve. Rules and guidelines, as one of us said, seem to 'drive the heart out' of what we do; they seem to form a system which renders us impotent and those with whom we are concerned anonymous.

This is for good reason and in no way invalidates the purpose of regulation. Law works in universals and generics: it applies (i) equally to all members of a category and (ii) consistently over time, and this is why we value it. But we are motivated as much by the lived experience of individual human beings as by legal and statistical constructs. Though we work in categories, what we know are cases – and all cases are in some way unique, special unto themselves. This is why so much work is involved in trying to establish the way in which this or that law applies to precisely this person in this situation, here and now.

What became clear in our discussion was that for human beings to be equal we will always need the ordinary, everyday, individual and collective judgment and commitment of other human beings. Indeed, we might think of much of the work of organisations and individuals engaged with inequalities as that of mediating between the rule and reality, the category and the case: we will remain advocates both for the standardising, equalising project of the law and for the enduring, individual and specific qualities of human beings. ☐

9. The inefficiencies of mainstreaming

Helen Chambers, Inspiring Scotland

> Scaling up successful interventions absorbs time and
> energy – and money – we can ill afford. Is there a way
> of making social and public policy more efficient as well
> as more effective?

AFTER decades of work we are still struggling to address
inequality in Scottish society and to see a significant improvement for the individuals and communities at its sharpest edge.
Why does policy seem so ineffective? I think it has something to
do with its inefficiency.

The current model of social policy development has a
beautiful, logical, simple elegance. It runs as follows: design an
intervention, evidence-based of course, rather than driven by
funding opportunities; evaluate it thoroughly, perhaps even in
economic terms; prove the intervention works, in terms of
measurable outcomes; take your evidence to funders/
purchasers/commissioners/procurers, who will recognise that
this intervention provides better results for the resources they
have available (using the robust benchmarking data they have
to hand). They will then withdraw funding from an existing
piece of work that has less successful outcomes, and scale and
expand the newly proven intervention.

We accept this model as a fundamental given, though many
participants recognise it as at best significantly flawed, if not
completely false. On a piece of work I have recently been

involved in, many hoops have been jumped through. The idea works. It is aligned to the current policy zeitgeist and strategic plans. It has been evaluated to death, including substantial economic analysis. To progress further, the team is now driven to behave as some sort of policy version of door-to-door encyclopedia salesmen. This intervention assists individuals and communities suffering some of our most rampant inequalities in a broad range of positive ways from health and employability outcomes, through to community cohesion and civic participation. To get it 'mainstreamed', we have to work hard to sell the idea and try to convince potential 'purchasers' – whether local or national government, discretionary grant funder, philanthropists – to jump on board so that the project starts reaching some scale.

'Scale' is an interesting concept. The original work reached ten vulnerable communities. In order to double its scope, taking it to eight new local authorities (our current aim), we have had over 70 meetings. To reach all 32 authorities and 14 Health Boards – well, as our American colleagues say, 'You do the math'.

All this promotional activity has to find a place among all the work that needs to be done to keep existing programmes up and running – and in some way, has to be paid for. The time it takes absorbs energy and attention which might otherwise be spent on keeping existing services running. In the current climate, which is one of cumulative layers of Community Planning Partnerships, Integrated Joint Boards and initiatives such as Thriving Places, among many others, Scotland's policy community is creating more and more complex webs of individuals, organisations and systems that need to be involved before decisions are taken. We have now created a world where motivated and committed individuals cannot collectively influence how public money is spent to really affect outcomes.

This matters, for three major reasons. Firstly, because it's expensive: negotiating and persuading take time and costs money, eating resources that could fund effective interventions. Secondly, because it makes for delay: the time-lag between discovering an effective intervention and getting it to some sort of scale entails real world, day-to-day distress, stress, damage, ill health (and in some cases mortality) of living, breathing human beings. I feel that in accepting such a sluggish model for change we have lost not just our common sense but our moral compass. Thirdly, we have created an environment where many of those expected to implement large scale change inevitably lack the sense of ownership, enthusiasm or understanding of those involved in the original initiative.

The consequence of this is that for decades very many, potentially significant, effective interventions fail to reach scale. The individuals promulgating them run out of funding, or energy. So we reinvent the wheel and go through the loop again, compounding the cost and time involved to make change. Even if some kind of expansion does take place, endless short-term funding cycles will drain its momentum and eventually kill the intervention. This can be very frustrating for all involved.

As a result of the Christie Commission and other bodies, Scotland's political and policy communities have recognised and accepted that we need to see a radical shift in spending from acute intervention to prevention. Yet nearly everything militates against this: institutional inertia, political discomfort, media responses, vested interests, and innate human discomfort around change and risk.

It is tempting to be brave and to offer a solution, but perhaps that might be missing the point completely. A key feature of most recent policy developments has been to involve those affected in the definition, design and resolution of the challenges that face them. A pre-designed response from a policy professional flies in the face of these approaches and would not just be ironic but offensive. So, in outlining a possible way forward, I offer a different type of provocation.

In order to speed up change, can we utilise established and verified methods such as citizens' juries and 'people's panels' to examine and resolve methods for making speedy financial commitment to evidence-based interventions? Change can often be stymied by real or perceived opposition from local communities. Rather than use citizens' juries on each and every topic (justice, safety and so on) or at each budgetary decision point, can we mutually agree a process that a community signs up to and which is then implemented on its behalf – with agreed and appropriate engagement? This avoids a massive absorption of time and energy from often very challenged individuals and communities and perhaps also provides a consensual way forward that moves towards a 'done with' model, rather than a 'done to' model. Once this agreement is in place it might be possible to, if not exactly 'fast track' proven interventions, at least implement them with some level of energy and momentum. It might also provide an environment where the principles underlying 'defunding' and other difficult choices can be discussed out of the heat of the moment rather than in respect of specific services or functions.

There may be many reasons why this proposal is not the right response. But for humanity's sake – and for our sanity, too – we need to find one fast. ☐

10. Policy talk

Madelaine Simpkin

Policy making is often thought of as being all about documents and decisions, but much of it is also woven with some form of talk: understanding and working with talk is a critical part of addressing inequality.

FOR a number of years now, policy – in the broadest sense, from conception to execution – has been on my radar as a potentially powerful tool for addressing matters of inequality. I have studied with interest particular policies such as: childcare accessibility and parental leave regulations aimed at facilitating women's ability to work; tax and redistribution legislation aimed at closing inequality gaps; or representation mandates aimed at increasing the presence of a wide cross-section of women in social and political life. Among the myriad of policies aimed at targeting aspects of inequality, there is an enormous amount of evidence to support nuanced, complex and intersectional implementation. And yet, these policies are rare to fully materialise in their imagined capacity.

Scores of academics and policymakers have puzzled over this problem: why *do* these policies repeatedly fail to be fully realised? There are case studies from all over the world. Some point to a lack of political commitment. Others point to a lack of resources. Others still cite structural constraints: the big institutions that frame our society – capitalism, global governance – do not work for everyone. Meanwhile, many practitioners will argue that most theorists trying to explain the impediments 'do not really understand' policy making and that the work of policy making is rarely captured in an accurate, grounded way.

There is a pervasive sense in both the field and academia that policy making ideally occurs in a linear and rational manner, with physical inscription at its core: legislation, reams of clinical meeting minutes, reports from commissions and working groups, and so forth. However, the documents and decision-making is encompassed by muddled sense-making and the explicit manifestation thereof: *talk*. That talk can be informal or formal, between many or between a few. It is almost always non-linear and, though unrecognised, it is the heartbeat sustaining policy making.

If we were to understand that talk is a vital part of the policy process, then perhaps we could begin by seriously prioritising and facilitating more productive forms of it. I often hear people in Scotland grumbling about 'talking shops' taking up all of our time, of meetings and email exchanges dragging on and taking away from the 'real' work. Those perspectives miss the point, I think. Those actions are significant aspects of the work. Arguably, much of the rest is some form of documentation.

To many this will seem obvious and mundane. To others it can be quite an uncomfortable concept: one need not look any further than our Reference Group which is providing the essays for this book. The purpose of the group was to talk and, as Darcy Leigh's essay pointed out, this was met with mixed levels of comfort and enthusiasm. And this makes sense. There is something quite rational in today's context about wanting to see an immediate connection between action and outcomes.

Our society is motivated by results, and process is secondary. For many, the abstractions of process are tiring and too nebulous to be effective.

But in trying to deal with our increasingly complex world, and in tackling intricate problems such as inequality, perhaps it is in the abstract that magic will occur. Perhaps talking to people, working out ideas and making them explicit, and making people accountable for how they come to see issues, are in fact the components that really facilitate substantive change.

We are beginning to see the idea of talking more infiltrating the way we work both in public and private sectors. Indeed, in Scotland, the role of the civil servant has changed dramatically over the past ten years. There is an increasing amount of attention given to getting people to collaborate in a number of ways, to break down silos, to radically reconsider working spaces. But is radical attention to issues of inequality at its core? Are we going far enough? How and why you bring people together has a direct effect on output: the topic, the facilitation, the space – it all matters.

Of course, many will say that prioritising talk is resource intensive. But talk happens as an intrinsic part of policymaking with or without intention. This means that it makes sense for us to focus on purposeful forms of talk. Perhaps, we might then draw out the stories behind people's understandings of policy problems and their potential solutions, keeping the ideas honest and open. Many of us know the importance of this intuitively but it would be helpful if we bring together the evidence base for the importance of talk in the policy process, and think creatively about how to talk in more productive ways.

History has given us clues about the potential of this method.

A civil servant recently reminded me that the Enlightenment did not happen on paper; it came about in coffee shops and other public fora and was powerful precisely because it was a period of exchanging and challenging ideas. We need a 21st century enlightenment, one which is deeply concerned about the insidious and pervasive inequalities that we continue to face. Talking will not be the only means of overcoming them, but it will allow us to go back to basics, shining light into dark corners, and drawing out the ideas that support meaningful, substantive change. ☐

11. Policy and voice

Elinor Mitchell, Scottish Government

The work of policy has changed. Policy making now is about listening and talking, trying to nurture an emergent future into being.

WHAT is the work of policy making in the civil service these days? It's certainly very different to what is was when I joined the civil service in 1988. Back then, we had quite clear roles within hierarchies, saw very little of Ministers, or stakeholders, and the flow of information was quite closely controlled and guarded. We consulted on a limited number of options, and wondered why our policies didn't always have the impact we expected. But we didn't really learn from those experiences, or reflect on the extent to which we and our ways of working and relating were contributing to the results we were seeing. And we (thought we) held most of the power; we took decisions and explained them later; we controlled access to information and shared what we wanted; and we were sufficiently removed from real people and communities that it was hard to make connections.

I've spent the vast majority of my career in the policy world and I can see that the way we go about our business has changed dramatically. Policy, at its simplest, is a description of how to meet the government's objectives. Policy has ideas in it, it sets out ways of working, contains evidence from the past and it should help everyone involved understand the desired outcome and direction of travel. How we develop policy is really important. We know that those affected by the circumstances we are trying to improve (like health inequalities, or poverty) know vital things about what will work to make them better. So we need to find ways to hear their voices and really understand the lived experience of people living the lives that we want to see improved. And that isn't about sharing some ideas and asking for comments – it is about getting out and about, listening deeply and asking questions, making connections and being curious and interested in how the policies and services provided are impacting on people's lives. It's also about reflecting on what we see and hear and thinking through, with others, how we might respond to what we see and hear.

And we civil servants sometimes find that quite challenging. We have a clear set of values – we must be honest, objective, impartial and act with integrity. And most of us feel, with a passion, the desire to make the world a better place, to improve people's lives, to make a difference, to be a positive force for change. And I've come to believe that the most important contribution I can make is to be a disrupter in the system. Why? Because the system we have is the one delivering the outcomes we achieve – and that just isn't good enough. And because I now recognise that inequality in power and voice is one of the most insidious and damaging of inequalities.

So, the role I see for myself, is disrupting the current way we do things – the accepted norms of who does what in our society, and whose voice matters most. That means accepting that I and my colleagues don't know the answers and trying (really hard) not to leap to action but instead getting alongside people, and listening. It also means bringing all of myself to conversations, being focused and interested and nurturing empathy. It means unleashing my curiosity – not feeling bound by job descriptions or roles but enjoying a freedom to roam and to explore the paths less taken. Some of us have been on the ULab journey – a programme of participatory discussion oriented to social change. One of the most powerful aspects for me is the notion of an emerging future because I can see that the world around us is changing at the most incredible speed, and things we previously thought were givens have disappeared. So for me there is a comfort in believing that we need to let go of much of what has gone before and work with a wide range of people, to think through and imagine a better, different future. Is that everyone's experience of how civil servants work? I guess not. There is a way to go, but I truly believe that the genie is out of the bottle and that there is no going back. □

III Politics

Our third section takes up the inescapably political nature of equalities and inequalities in Scotland, and engages with the continuing significance of class, race and gender.

Gerry McCartney sets the terms of political debate, pointing to the need for public intervention and collective mobilisation. Jatin Haria tries to understand why public awareness of black and minority ethnic populations in Scotland is still so limited, and why racism goes unacknowledged. Meryl Kenny makes the case for quotas to increase the representation of women in our formal political institutions. Ann Henderson, similarly, argues that continuing vigilance is needed to promote and protect the interests of women in the workplace.

Fergus McMillan describes the work that needs to be done to realise equality in respect of sexuality and sexual identity, and Fiona McHardy shows how much can be done when those most affected by inequalities are supported in documenting and promoting discussion of them.

12. Political action on inequality

Gerry McCartney, Scottish Public Health Observatory

Achieving greater equity in Scotland will require legislation and taxation, a comprehensive approach across different domains, the political mobilisation of those most affected and making the case to others that they, too, will benefit.

SCOTLAND is a profoundly unequal nation. Where and to whom you were born has an enormous influence on the rest of your life. For example, women born in the most affluent 10 per cent of Scottish areas can expect to live an extra 23 years in good health than those living in the most deprived 10 per cent of areas. Amongst men, the difference is 24 years. These inequalities are evident as a gradient across the whole population, with each group except the most affluent having progressively worse outcomes.

Inequalities in income, wealth and health have not always been this stark. Between the 1920s and 1970s in Britain there was a dramatic reduction in inequalities. This coincided with the creation of the welfare state (including the NHS, council housing and numerous other public services) driven by a strong and organised working class who had lived through two devastating world wars and imagined a different future. By the late 1970s however the tide had turned. The welfare state was rolled back, industry was closed or privatised, taxes reduced and social, economic and health inequalities rapidly increased once again such that they are now back at the same level that they were in the 1920s. Health inequalities in Scotland are now larger than in the rest of Western and Central Europe on some measures.

These stark inequalities have not gone unnoticed. During the 2014 Independence Referendum the extent of inequality was the regular subject of debate with both sides arguing that their constitutional arrangements would be the most effective for promoting equity. This debate was informed by a vast amount of research looking at the international evidence base at the types of policies most effective at reducing inequality. It shows that policies and interventions which use legislation, regulation and taxation were much more likely to be effective than those reliant on individual agency or behaviour change.

The Scottish Public Health Observatory published work at this time comparing a range of policy approaches to reducing health inequalities. It used the best available evidence of who is exposed to a range of factors, the likely reach of different interventions and policies, and their size of effect. It compared the impacts on a common set of outcomes – inequalities in mortality and hospitalisation – alongside the costs of the interventions. This showed that increasing the minimum wage, increasing income tax and creating employment were all likely to have large positive effects, measures encouraging behaviour change had much smaller effects and increasing regressive taxes had negative impacts. Further work is currently underway to expand the range of interventions modelled and the number of outcomes across which these can be compared.

Equality is usually understood as everyone receiving the same, while equity can be defined as resources being distributed across society according to the different needs of individuals and

61

groups. Creating the context in which equity can flourish is important – and requires a comprehensive approach. Focusing on child poverty, educational attainment or unemployment is important, but even effective actions on any of these is unlikely to be sufficient. Instead, supportive policies across a full range of domains in Scottish society is likely to be required. There are many areas which have received less attention in Scotland, perhaps because they carry less popular support or because they require challenging those with power more directly.

For example, little attention has been given recently to the inequalities that arise in the education system as a result of the existence of fee-paying schools or as a result of the differences in house prices across schools' catchment areas. The opportunities that public, worker or co-operative ownership of industry present are rarely discussed, nor is the dramatic rise in privately rented accommodation – presumably because these would require challenging the revenue streams enjoyed by vocal and influential groups of voters. This cuts to the core of the challenge of reducing inequality. In the short-run, those with most to lose are those in the most powerful positions. Indeed, many of those who might use their influence to reduce inequalities are compromised by their own use of private education, ownership of rental houses or company shares.

There are two lessons from this finding. First, achieving equity is more likely if those with the most to gain have an effective voice. In the past this has been achieved through the trade unions and their elected representatives at national and local level, the tenants' movement and co-operatives; all supported by conscience-raising activities and struggle. Clearly these structures do not have the strength or reach that they once had, and finding ways of organising the shared interests of those who have least in today's society more effectively is urgently needed. Second, the case has to be made to those currently benefiting most from inequality that greater equity is also in their interest.

The work of Kate Pickett and Richard Wilkinson is important in this regard as they have demonstrated that more equal nations have better outcomes for the whole of society. There are a number of possible reasons for this. The stresses of living in unequal societies, even for the most affluent is damaging. The affluent have to absorb the social costs of repairing the consequences of inequality (including greater crime, pollution and worse health). They also spend time and money to avoid the poor, in terms of their housing, education for their children and in obtaining services. Achieving greater equity therefore requires both a stronger voice and demonstrable power for the most disadvantaged and building a greater understanding of the most affluent that equity is also in their interests.

Policy can help to achieve these goals. Using the tax system more progressively and reducing wage differentials is required. Universal public services give everyone a stake in them being high quality and well-funded. Restricting alternatives which allow the most affluent to bypass the system could make this even more effective. □

13. Jock Tamson's bairns

Jatin Haria, Coalition for Racial Equality and Rights

Statistics show that race inequalities are a continuing feature of today's Scotland, though public discourse suggests otherwise. Greater public awareness and political pressure is needed to address these inequalities with the urgency they deserve.

AS the well-known Scottish saying goes, 'We're all Jock Tamson's bairns'. The perceived notion of Scotland is that of a country with a strong history in protecting the rights and freedoms of everyone, a country where respect, protection and promotion of equality and human rights is intrinsic in its very nature. But does the reality match the rhetoric?

One of the key reasons given historically for a 'no problem here' attitude is the relatively low number of black/minority ethnic people (BME) in Scotland. The small number was probably true a decade or two ago – the 1991 census showed a BME population of just 1.25%, rising to just 2 per cent in the 2001 Census. However, the 2011 Census records a BME population of 4 per cent overall, with Glasgow recording a BME population of 12 per cent, and Aberdeen 8 per cent. Indeed the black/minority ethnic population of Glasgow is now similar to that of the UK average and higher than that of cities such as Liverpool. The excuse of small numbers, which was never relevant but one that allowed people to ignore the reality of racism experienced by those 'small' BME communities in Scotland, no longer adds up at any level.

Other reasons that often feature in the 'no problem' account are that sectarianism is a far bigger problem to be dealt with or, at the very least, that we in Scotland are not as bad as those in England. Either or both of these statements may or may not be true but are not in any way an appropriate response to the reality of racism in Scotland.

Police Scotland recorded a total of 5,520 crimes as part of a racist incident in 2013-14. However, studies suggest that nearly half of all incidents do not get formally reported. Most perpetrators are young white men who have recently left school, and as such it is no surprise that some 3,000 racist incidents have been reported *in* Scottish schools since 2011.

Even more worrying, the Institute of Race Relation's Factfile on Racially Motivated Murders (Known or Suspected) between 2000 and 2014 lists 10 victims from Scotland, out of 80 in total. Many of these have had little if any media interest, and are too often seen as 'one-off' incidents rather than a broader reflection on Scottish society. Indeed, a decade after the Macpherson Inquiry, the then Scottish Justice Secretary Kenny MacAskill, addressing SEMPERscotland (Scotland's equivalent of the National Black Police Association) had made the bold statement that 'institutional racism does not exist in the police service in Scotland – of that I'm sure'. If such complacency exists in senior politicians it is no wonder that the rest of Scottish society follows suit.

And the problem is not just of actual racial attacks or the criminal justice system. For example, despite 50 years of legislation aimed at tackling racial inequality, black/minority ethnic people in Scotland are still twice as likely to live in poverty compared to their white counterparts, and although most black/

minority ethnic pupils achieve better school qualifications, unemployment is around three times higher for some ethnic minority groups compared to most white ethnic groups.

In 2011/12, just 2.1 per cent of BME applicants for local authority jobs were appointed compared to 6.1 per cent of white UK applicants. Even after interviews, where it could be assumed that people meeting shortlisting requirements were equally qualified and experienced, BME candidates were still only half as likely to be appointed as their white counterparts. If this situation is allowed to continue then the ethnic penalty faced by black/ minority ethnic people in Scotland will only continue to grow.

In terms of political representation (before the 2017 local elections), outside of Glasgow, there were just 10 BME local councillors (out of a total of 1143), with 25 of Scotland's 32 local authority areas having no BME representatives – including our capital city, Edinburgh. Just four of the 1222 local councillors in Scotland were black women. If the number reflected the proportion of black/minority ethnic women in Scotland, there would be around 24.

Despite the clear evidence, discussion of racism (beyond its intersection with immigration) is largely off the agenda for the reasons outlined above, and any outrage at racial discrimination in Scotland is primarily now restricted to 'celebrity' racism scandals and commentary on social media. This allows people to feel as though they oppose racism without actually having to do anything to address it in their own lives.

All this reflects a very limited understanding of what racism really is and detracts from the real structuring power of racism. We seem to have moved on to a post-racial society without acknowledging that 'race' was ever an issue. A key factor that allows ongoing inequalities such as those outlined above to continue is the lack of pressure on public bodies and wider Scottish society to take real meaningful action to achieve change. This needs Scotland to have a better understanding of racism and for more people to play their part in actively challenging it, whether this is institutional racism or everyday racism.

Scotland in 2017 has well-meaning people and policies, but the denial that there is a problem here inevitably results in a lack of action, with no sense of urgency in dealing with the issue. What is required is for those who currently hold power to share that power with people who have previously been denied and disadvantaged by it. Is Scotland up for that challenge? ☐

14. Women in politics: why quotas matter

Meryl Kenny, University of Edinburgh

One way of assessing women's presence in the formal institutions of parliamentary politics is simply by counting them. This suggests that quotas are essential to their achieving political equality.

WHO runs the world? The short answer: men do. Despite a global upwards trend in women's representation, 77 per cent of parliamentarians worldwide are male. Only 32 per cent of the House of Commons are women, a stark figure highlighted by a succession of reports in recent years on women's continuing under-representation in British politics. The Scottish Parliament does not fare much better. Only 35 per cent of its MSPs are female, a drop since devolution.

What can be done about this democratic deficit? Backed by a large body of international evidence, increasingly the call in Scotland and the UK is for tough measures in the form of statutory gender quotas that require all parties to take action on women's representation. Quotas are simply a type of equality measure that require an increase in the number or proportion of particular parliamentarians and/or make a particular social characteristic a necessary qualification for office. On this dimension, quotas deliver– the international evidence over-whelmingly finds that well-designed and properly implemented quotas are the most effective way of ensuring significant increases in women's numerical presence in political institutions. But beyond this, quotas entail a more fundamental challenge to gendered power inequalities – not only in terms of the distribution of political positions, but also, potentially, resulting in attitudinal, cultural and behavioural shifts, and/or substantive changes in political 'ways of working' and policy outcomes.

For some, though, debates over women's (under)represent-ation and gender quotas construct the problem of political inequality in ways that are too limited. They are too preoccupied with inclusion and 'counting numbers' at the expense of trans-formative change, and too focused on formal political instit-utions at the expense of other important channels of represent-ation. Others point to the lack of recognition of differences amongst women, and the need for representational reform strategies that cut across intersecting identities, rather than treat 'women' as a monolithic group. Merely 'counting' women, for example, doesn't reveal to us the fact that there has never been a woman of colour elected to the Scottish Parliament.

These are important arguments. Nevertheless, 'counting' remains an important *element* of addressing inequality in political institutions, highlighting gendered power relations and providing evidence of discriminatory practices that continue to affect women's and men's lives. In a simple act of counting, for example, Rosie Campbell and Sarah Childs demonstrated that 45 per cent of women MPs in the House of Commons had no children, compared to 28 per cent of male MPs. Considering the intersection between 'sex' and parenthood in this way is obviously a simplification that doesn't fully capture variations in family structure, but the stark differences do show us that power structures still serve as a barrier to the presence of people who identify as women and are parents in the UK Parliament.

Counting is also an effective way of politicising the under-representation of women (and other marginalised groups) and of holding political actors to account. Indeed, many political parties and institutions still don't count for themselves. The Westminster Parliament Speaker's Conference on parliamentary representation which reported in 2010 recommended that parties be required to report candidate gender and ethnicity breakdowns every six months, and that parties should publish a gender/diversity breakdown, together with targets. The requirement for parties to publish candidate diversity data is now in place in Section 106 of the Equality Act 2010, but this provision has not yet been brought into force. And while individual parties and leaders have committed to providing such data, these promises have been only periodically and incompletely delivered upon, and frequently only after significant internal and external pressure (a criticism raised again in Sarah Childs's recent *Good Parliament* report). Requiring actors to regularly count for themselves would help ensure transparency and accountability, whilst also providing further insights into the nature of the 'problem' of political inequality and under-representation, and the pathways that different groups take to power.

Why does it matter? Symbolically, women's political inequality matters for democratic legitimacy and public engagement. Increasing women's presence in political institutions affects how others – particularly (but not exclusively) women – perceive these institutions and their place in them. Moreover, parliaments and legislatures remain an important (but not the only) site of political representation, as demonstrated by the extensive body of work on the importance of women and feminist legislators as 'critical actors' in effecting change. Rather than lay all the responsibility for combatting inequality at the feet of women representatives or women's civil society organisations we also need to ask questions about the kinds of accountability mechanisms, institutions and relationships that exist to hold government and other policy actors to account with regards to gender inequality. In Scotland, for example, action on domestic violence policy – a significant achievement of the first Scottish Parliament and Scottish Executive – was facilitated by the political leadership of women ministers and MSPs, but also by the institutionalised input of women's organisations into the policy process, as well as by new accountability structures and relationships, including regular reporting and other parliamentary mechanisms.

Quotas alone, then, are not a cure-all for women's political inequality. They need to be appropriately designed and effectively implemented and enforced in order to make a difference. And they do not in themselves remove all obstacles to equal political representation; they need to be situated within a wider strategy aimed at reforming recruitment and selection practices, targeting attitudes, and changing institutional cultures and processes. But they are a necessary first step that is required to achieve equality in our political institutions. ☐

15. Visibility and vigilance

Ann Henderson, Scottish TUC

> Women fought for a political presence in the workplace,
> but are often rendered invisible in discussions of work
> and employment. Only constant vigilance can ensure
> women workers are recognised and their needs
> addressed.

SIX women attended the 1911 STUC Congress in Dundee. As far as we know, with the exception of Margaret Irwin, who attended the founding Congress as a delegate from the Scottish Council of Women's Trades, this was the first time there had been a number of women delegates. Jeanie Spence, Mrs Lamont, Agnes Brown, Mary MacArthur, Kate McLean and Rachel Devine are names to be remembered.

These six women at the Congress all had proud records, leading struggles which shaped everyone's working lives as the Government then established Wages Boards. Despite the terrible conditions in which women worked – poor sanitation, no adjustments for pregnancy, long hours, working with all sorts of chemicals – women were not initially recognised as fit to be Factory Inspectors. Early evidence suggests that they organised to speak up in this role anyway, whether recognised or not.

Women also led the fight in local communities for decent housing, for mother and baby clinics, for decent nutrition for their families. It was 1928 before women secured the right to vote on the same terms as men, yet significant changes were made in working women's lives through the efforts of women such as those who attended the early STUC Congresses. But this doesn't feature in the image of trade unions held by most of us.

In 1917, 100 years ago, during the First World War, Mark Starr, a miner in Wales, wrote that 'while women's entrance into industry may – especially if the male workers do not tackle the problem intelligently – at first have disastrous results, still, if she finally gains economic independence and becomes the true equal and comrade of man, undreamt of beneficial results will accrue.' Though the problem recognised continues today, we can surely find a way to resolve it, for if we don't, inequality – of which invisibility is a part – will persist.

The trade union movement is still seen by many as a predominantly male preserve, organising and speaking for men at work. This hampers the ability of the movement to grow and better represent all for whom it should speak.

Here are the facts on recent trade union membership in Scotland. The Scottish TUC's 2015 membership figures record a total membership from all affiliated unions of 596,303. Of this, roughly 51.3 per cent were women, and 48.7 per cent men. That year, the STUC General Council, elected at Congress, composed of 39 members, 21 of whom were women (54 per cent). We work with women who are employed in every sector of the economy and achieve amazing results as they represent, and organise in, their workplaces.

Alongside these facts, however, there are frequent moments of invisibility, or at least, that is how it feels. Here are some examples taken from the past year or so.

On 12 June 2016, a prominent trade union leader was quoted in the *Sunday Herald*: 'Scottish society is scarred by huge inequality. One of the key ways that you address inequality is by having an economy that creates jobs. For working class people, that's proper apprenticeships and manufacturing type jobs'. This appears to render invisible 46 per cent of this particular trade union's membership, which is to be found primarily in the public sector, in retail and in care, as well as some women within manufacturing. But even more than that, the wider discussion of 'proper' jobs can leave many of those in the precarious workforce feeling ignored and poorly represented.

Similarly, a newspaper headline on the consequences of the centralisation of the Scottish Fire Service – 'Firemen Fury as 1,000 Scots jobs go' – suggests the loss of jobs held mostly by men. Whilst there are still significantly more men than women employed in the Fire Service, in fact a far greater proportion of the jobs lost were posts held by women, such as those of skilled local control room call operators.

Meanwhile, a major commitment has been given by the SNP, reflected in the Scottish Government's programme for 2016 onwards, to expand and invest in early years and childcare. This is a massive boost to the economy and will be of significant benefit to children and families. With a projected increase of over 18,000 Full Time Equivalent (FTE) posts, this deserves a headline or two. This is a huge opportunity to improve the diversity of the workforce, to raise wages and employment conditions across the sector, to create new career paths and job security for those currently employed and those of the future. The jobs that are needed are varied, and include early years and childcare practitioners, teachers, cleaners, catering staff, janitors, and all that goes with building the infrastructure.

Also needed are other health professionals and skilled support staff, to meet the needs of all children, young people and their families, in all of Scotland's communities.

Yet headlines on this are hard to find on the Scottish Government's website. Press releases proudly announce 150 new jobs with the contract for a new ferry at Ferguson Marine Engineering (31 August 2015), 150 at new commercial units in Strathclyde Business Park (7 October 2015) and 50 arising from the Commonwealth Games with the opening of the Dalmarnock Legacy Hub (9 October 2015). 'Proper jobs' are made visible but jobs in an ambitious transformational expansion of the early years, childcare and out of school care sector are not.

There are big questions to be addressed in developing policy and economic strategies. The Scottish Government Early Years and Childcare Strategic Forum brings together a wealth of experience from education, regulatory bodies, providers, local authorities, the STUC, voluntary sector, academia, and the Scottish Government. These are strong voices speaking on behalf of a sector which has a mainly female workforce.

But visibility is about what we all choose to say, see and hear. One hundred years on from Mark Starr's observations, we have still to find the right way of achieving that equality in which 'undreamt of beneficial results will accrue'. Women are to be found at every level of our trade unions, in every sector and in every policy area. They are women of colour, with disabilities, and of different ages. We need to be vigilant in keeping them visible. ☐

16. Achieving LGBT equality

Fergus McMillan, LGBT Youth Scotland

> LGBT young people face barriers in their personal, community, school and working lives. Addressing the resultant inequalities requires legislation, community-based work and individual support.

THE vision of LGBT Youth Scotland, working with lesbian, gay, bisexual and transgender (LGBT) young people for the past nearly thirty years, is to remove the barriers – barriers caused by decades of prejudice and discrimination – so that all LGBT young people enjoy equality in the law and, above all, liberation as equal human beings. This has involved campaigning, community-based work, and support for individuals.

There has been a sustained campaign for equal rights for LGBT people over the past 20 years, with almost complete transformation in the law, from the repeal of Section 2a of the Local Government Act (Section 28) in 2000, to workplace and education protections for LGBT people and the rights of transsexual people to have their gender legally recognised. This is within a context of wider equality and human rights legislation such as the Children and Young People (Scotland) Act 2014, the Equality Act 2010 and its Public Sector Equality Duties requiring all those in the public sector to eliminate unlawful discrimination, harassment and victimisation, advance equality of opportunity and foster good relations. These legislative drivers support preventative work, for example, when challenging homophobic, biphobic and transphobic bullying or when young people approach us to say that work to address inequality isn't happening or is being blocked in their school community.

LGBT Youth Scotland also works in partnership to improve public services and make local communities more inclusive of LGBT people. Good practice in leadership, practice and policy is encouraged through the *LGBT Charter of Rights* programme for organisations in the public, third and soon to be private sectors. The professional standards of several professions, such as those of the General Teaching Council and Community Learning and Development (CLD) Standards Council, also play a role in ensuring that policy feeds into practice. The resulting interactions between personal beliefs and affiliations, organisational policy, professional regulation and legislation provides space for professional dialogue and the development of good practice. Legislation and regulation are thus important in addressing inequality, particularly where prejudice and discrimination is overt and tolerated.

Just as important, but perhaps less visible, is the role of youth work in connecting young people to their communities around them, whether that be a school community, local community, the country in which they live, or their 'thematic community' (LGBT community, or feminism). For LGBT Youth Scotland, that's involved supporting young people to speak out on issues that matter to them and have their voices heard. The equal marriage campaign in Scotland was a true success story in terms of the inclusion of young people in legislative and social change.

The task of working with a group of young people for whom their surrounding community might not be a safe place to be, by virtue of their own emerging or developed identity, and who need help in redressing the balance of years of structural and institutional prejudice and discrimination, is complex. Young people should not have to address that discrimination on their own (as previous generations have had to do). Partnership – individual, inter-generational and organisational – has been central to my vision for how we create sustainable long-term change for all young people. A recent example involved a young person in residential childcare who experienced homophobia, not only from other young people but also from staff. Youth workers at LGBT Youth Scotland worked with the young person to address the issues with staff, which resulted in him delivering LGBT awareness raising training, with his youth worker, for all staff and other young people where he lived.

An organisation such as LGBT Youth Scotland can reach out to young people from a range of communities, rural and urban, affluent and economically poor, and work with the day to day lived-reality of young people's lives, however complex that might be. At its core is the reality that inequality is experienced by people in multiple forms, sometimes referred to as 'intersect-ional inequality', for example, the intersection of poverty and LGBT identity. We can also harness the commitment of people with particular skills who understand the dynamics of inequality and the often subtle, but damaging, effects it can have on a young person's well-being and life chances.

We can work both with the individual young person in front of us, and seek to change the environment around them. These two aspects of our work combine powerfully with each other. The impact of the campaign and eventual change in the law to make same-sex marriage legal in Scotland was positive in legal terms and in social attitudes towards LGBT people in Scotland. An important further benefit was that individual young people who took part in the campaign grew in terms of their own social and political capital.

In this way legislation can help both in securing equal rights and also in influencing social attitudes, but I believe strongly that some of the more profound and intractable inequalities, like inequality in our culture and the ethos of institutions is effectively changed by exposure to the day to day lived-realities of people. This can be done through awareness training, culture and inclusion, and by embracing difference. Each individual young person's experience involves very specific challenges arising from their own context, the people close to them, their family relationships, and the language used. This is illustrated very clearly in another of the *Postcards from Scotland* series – *He, She, They*. In this book, Shirley Young tells the moving story of her daughter Jane's transition to his adult identity as Nathan. This was not just a journey for Nathan, but for the family and for others around them, a story of emotionally intense experiences for all involved. In his 'afterword' to the book, Nathan explains the importance of individual stories:

> When my mum first raised the idea of writing a book
> about the impact of my transition on our family I
> instinctively said yes. I don't feel I have ownership of
> our story. It's just as much mum's to tell as it is mine.
> The idea of our family's experience being out there
> for other people to read excited me for another
> reason: I think it's important for us all to hear various
> stories about trans people's lives.

Even though the legislative and regulatory framework is in place, young people still experience bullying and prejudice. Sustainable change requires programmes that seek to change culture, to dismantle barriers and prevent discrimination, but we also need to support individual young people in their developing understanding and experience of their gender identity and sexual orientation. ☐

17. Doing research, doing politics

Fiona McHardy, Poverty Alliance

With an increasing focus on evidence based policy, there is a need to reflect on how we collect evidence on inequality and poverty and the lived experience of it.

WHEN we talk about inequality a question is often asked about how we listen to the voices of people experiencing the consequences of inequality and facing poverty. Might evidence of lived experience be able to influence and drive change?

Currently we are seeing a shift in policy making in Scotland toward co-production and participation, with the Christie Commission highlighting the need for services to be co-designed with communities. In legislative terms, too, the introduction of the Community Empowerment Act provides new opportunities for influence with a focus on harnessing the assets of local communities.

On the ground, however, for those living on a low income, a challenging labour market and changing social security provision create increasing pressures on their day-to-day lives. In this context, it becomes increasingly important that it is not business as usual in policy making, that instead we take the opportunity to reflect and understand just what people's lived experiences are. We need to collect evidence from new forms of community research, and to use this knowledge for more effective policy making.

I write as a researcher involved in several pieces of community participatory research supporting people experiencing poverty. This article is based on lessons from several projects, including one facilitated in partnership with Fife Gingerbread, a community organisation and family support initiative.

This project brought together a group of ten female lone parents in Fife to conduct a piece of research on an issue that was important to them. The group represented a diverse range of circumstances – some were living in private rented accommodation, some were in social housing and others had more insecure circumstances; some had children with disabilities, some were experiencing long term physical or mental ill health; all were experiencing living on a low income.

The research process became a shared focus for understanding lived experiences and the commonalities and differences between them. Facilitated training sessions provided an opportunity for talking through the details of daily lives, identifying both barriers and enabling structures and systems. Collectively, through the project, we were able to create an evidence base, grounded and shaped by households directly experiencing poverty.

When published, this evidence provided an important example of the value and impact of well-resourced community research. This small group worked for 14 months to help produce the report 'Surviving Poverty – the Impact of Lone Parenthood', which was used in a range of policy settings including by MSPs in debates within the Scottish Parliament on welfare reform and child benefit, as well as to support successful funding applications for intervention projects in Fife. Its reach extended beyond Scotland to a House of Lords debate on welfare reform. Reflecting on these dissemination routes leads us to key factors that enhance and constrain the role of community-based research in tackling poverty and inequality in Scotland.

There are several advantages to using a community-based approach. It extends our understanding of social issues and challenges which are often obscured by conventional research methods. It creates opportunities to harness and build the assets and capacities of individuals and communities. It makes for the empowerment of otherwise passive research participants. It supports the development of policies that will be 'owned' by their intended beneficiaries – that is, by those who are invariably excluded from the process of evidence-based policy making.

Despite its obvious benefits, this approach is not without its complexity. Defining communities of interest and the mechanisms by which they might be represented demands careful consideration. Applying an intersectional lens to all stages of the process enhances the value and application of community-based research and the policy solutions that emerge from it.

Community research, like all research, is not produced in a vacuum but in an evolving and changing policy world. It requires policy makers to be open to receiving and hearing – and acting upon – research that may be challenging. It has to situate and position itself against competing research and policy priorities. Frameworks and funding streams need to adapt to support it – and it may raise issues quite different from traditional streams of thought. It require champions and an active programme of dissemination and campaigning across disciplines and policy domains. □

IV People

Our discussion often turned to the stories of people we had known and worked with. They turned on the recurrent theme of how we are brought into relation with each other, and how our relationships might be revisited and renewed.

In this final section, Ewan Aitken tells us about Tommy, Freddie and Grace, and how some of the worst manifestations of their inequality and isolation were overcome by their forming new relationships with others. Celine Sinclair introduces us to Amanda and Jonah, who live with disabilities, and their own and their families' difficulties in securing access to the provision to which they are entitled. Jamie Livingstone takes us elsewhere, to Mapira in Malawi as well as to Glasgow's Govan. In both contexts, it is communities which are crucial in working to overcome inequality. Diarmaid Lawlor takes us to Pennywell, a deprived community in Edinburgh seeking to learn from others in Germany. Caroline Gibb tells us about Susie, Louise and Mary, and the changes which had taken in place in their lives when they were invited into communities, and in turn began to engage with others.

18. Let me tell you about Tommy

Ewan Aitken, Cyrenians

Inequality is essentially about the obstacles that damage individual human beings and prevent them becoming the people they can be. Removing those obstacles and healing the damage requires people willing to share the journey.

EQUALITY is not about how many of anything we should each have or how wealthy we each should be. It is about the quality of opportunities we each have to flourish as human beings and our ability to make the best of them. Flourishing takes many forms and is nurtured in many ways. Flourishing happens when we experience a sense of belonging and meaning, purpose and identity. When opportunities to flourish are limited, damaged or removed then inequality at its deepest and most human form occurs.

Neuroscientists argue that our experience of flourishing is the result of varying quantities of endorphins (which come through exercise), dopamine (when we have a sense of achievement), serotonin (when we feel appreciated) and oxytocin (when we feel loved, lovable and that others will receive our love). While these chemical connections are central, I would argue that our minds and our soul (by which I mean our sense of inner well-being, not simply some religious definition), our consciousness of ourselves, is much more than the balance of chemicals in our brain.

The great Scottish Enlightenment thinker David Hume argued

'reason is but a slave to the passions'. We first respond to our experience of the world through our emotions and then use our minds to make sense of how we feel. Inequality is often a manifestation of limitations in a person's capacity to make that inner connection from emotion to reason, leading to decisions and choices that inhibit flourishing. For example, we know from research that the consequences of adverse childhood experiences such as poverty, neglect, trauma, and violence can bring huge limitations to a person's capacity to move beyond any response to the world outside other than the fundamental emotions of fight, flight or freeze.

Yet healing is possible when relationships are built and journeys are shared, when experiences happen in the safe spaces of what the Lankelly Chase Foundation call 'trusted, consistent and empathetic relationships' – relationships where we connect at an everyday as well as at a professional level.

Let me tell you about Tommy, an alcoholic who had, over 20 years, lost everything: family, home, job, friends. He was referred to Cyrenians as a supported volunteer on our Good Food FareShare programme redistributing surplus supermarket food to feed homeless and vulnerable people. When I met him he told me he'd been dry for three years, kept his tenancy for all that time, which was the longest he'd ever stayed in one place as an adult, and was back talking to his daughter. He told me that he discovered the strength to change when he discovered that volunteering with us meant he could be a helper rather than someone who was always needing helped.

Freddie, an older man, had lost the confidence to go out. His health was suffering and he was in danger of losing his home like many other socially isolated older people. Freddie was allocated one of our befrienders who asked him what he'd like to do. 'I want to vote in the referendum – in person', was the reply. 'That would make me feel part of life again, feel normal'. Over the following weeks the befriender and Freddie practised the walk, going a little further each time till the distance between Freddie's house and the polling booth was achieved. Freddie did vote in the referendum, but the really significant moment was when he met an old friend he'd not seen for over 20 years. They struck up where they had left off, they see each other every week and life just seems much better given a rekindled relationship made possible by the journey of trust travelled by the befriender and Freddie.

Grace was a school refuser. Her family life was chaotic and she didn't believe she amounted to anything. She was referred to Cyrenians' Key to Potential programme which offers six to nine months' support for young people in 3rd year who are struggling at school. After some early resistance to coming out from under the duvet, Grace expressed a desire to learn gaming programming. With support from Cyrenians and the school, she got on the course and is doing well. But the significant moment for Grace happened not when she got the place at college but when she did a placement with people with learning difficulties; she came back saying she wanted to create games for those who had much less than she did. Grace's journey took her to places in herself she had not explored. In trusting those she travelled with, she saw herself in a totally new light.

Cyrenians see our task as being simply to journey with those we serve, so they can find the spaces to discover in themselves the strength and resilience to be who they can be. The tipping points described here (being a helper for once, reigniting an old friendship, igniting a passion for serving others' needs) were all moments when those on the journey responded to a change they experienced in their inner lives; when they were ready, on their terms, in their time. It wasn't simply that their material or other external circumstances had changed: their inner well was filled again and the move from exclusion to inclusion had begun.

Cyrenians believe that the journey from exclusion to inclusion is first and foremost an inner journey, a journey of the human spirit, the soul. Yet, though it is an individual journey each person must take himself or herself, it is not a journey taken alone, but a journey of connectedness. We are all individuals but we are not autonomous beings, ever to be alone. It is in the quality of our relationships that we first find out who we are and what matters to us. It's all about relationships. Our capacity to be in a relationship – to be loved and to believe that others will receive our love – is central to whether we find ourselves feeling on the edge or included in life.

It is in that inner place where the debate about equality and inequality should begin and be framed. □

19. Every child

Celine Sinclair, The Yard

Scotland has a strong framework of laws on equalities and the rhetoric of statutory agencies is full of positive intentions. But the lived experience of individuals, such as the young people and their families who use The Yard, shows that this is not enough.

THE Edinburgh based charity The Yard runs adventure play centres supporting disabled children and young people and their families through play, youth and respite sessions. Our shared space allows families to meet others who face the same or similar challenges raising children with additional support needs (ASN). As an organisation, we therefore see and hear on a daily basis where a disconnect exists between the legislation, resulting policy and guidance designed to promote inclusion and equality, and the actual experience of the child and family.

The overarching legislation that is designed to prevent discrimination on the grounds of disability is the Equality Act (2010). The legislation makes it unlawful to discriminate against disabled people in relation to employment, the provision of goods and services, education and transport. In Scotland, an additional statute, the Education (Additional Support for Learning) (Scotland) Act 2004 supports disabled children. The concept of 'additional support needs' refers to any child or young person who, for whatever reason, requires additional support for learning. This may include challenges such as social, emotional, cognitive, linguistic, disability, or family and care circumstances. The level and type of support is determined by how these factors affect the individual child's learning. The legislation requires education authorities to make adequate and efficient provision for *every* child or young person.

The legislation is clearly well intentioned, but families report that the provision is neither flexible enough nor in many cases individual enough to result in a positive experience for their child. Many Scottish children, including many we see every day, are not being effectively included in many settings. Scotland's approach of Getting it Right for Every Child (GIRFEC) works for *most* but by no means *every* child in Scotland. At The Yard, we witness the cost to the individual, as the following case studies illustrate.

Amanda is 14 and has high functioning autism. Her experience in mainstream school has been, in the main, negative. She is socially isolated in a large and confusing environment and, although academically very able, she has not made the all-important friendships that are key to the success of a teenager. Her experience has been one of loneliness, depression, self-loathing and low self-esteem. There have been times when she has not attended school for over a year.

As a result, Amanda has experienced high levels of anxiety and required referral to Child and Adolescent Mental Health Services (CAMHS). Waiting lists for treatment in Scotland are lengthy and the delay can lead to children and young people reaching crisis point before they can access the support they need. The interface between the services needed to support Amanda and her family are complicated to navigate and the stress for the whole family has taken them to breaking point. Mum can no longer work as Amanda cannot attend school for prolonged periods of time. It may require court action against the local authority to secure alternative and more suitable provision.

This is not an isolated case. There are numerous cases in Scotland where children with ASN miss significant periods of school. Children and families in such situations report difficulties accessing information, long waiting lists and the need to fight to secure support. On paper and in law, these families have rights – but the reality is that these rights are not always provided automatically. Some families are better able to secure the resources required to meet their needs than others.

The principles behind The Education (ASL) Act are admirable. The intention is to create a fairer, more equitable and more tolerant society which supports all children. However, the presumption that children will be educated within mainstream schools, even where this is against parental wishes, meets the reality of limited funding and a lack of suitable additional support. Overall, there are more positive experiences than negative but these problems highlight the need for choice and access to information as well as emotional support for both child and family.

Jonah's experience of education has been more successful. Jonah has autism and mild learning difficulties and attends a language unit attached to a mainstream school. This model appears to work well. It provides some opportunities for inclusion whilst still allowing Jonah to benefit from the specialist teaching in a class of six and in an environment that is more suited to the sensory challenges he experiences as a result of his autism. After school, however, only unsuitable mainstream care is available. As a result, Jonah's mum, a chartered accountant, can no longer work as few employers allow employees to work from 9.30 until 2.00 with 13 weeks school holidays. This affects all aspects of family life, including housing and income.

In Scotland, we have committed to improving access to early education and play, yet we continue to build play spaces which are inaccessible and exclude disabled children who have fewer opportunities for both indoor and outdoor play. We still lack a consistent, comprehensive and inclusive approach and some children are therefore denied the well- evidenced and positive benefits of play. Poor access to play and leisure can lead directly to social isolation, lack of confidence and result in poor mental health. Amanda and Jonah have the same rights to education, fun and friendship as all children and accordingly should have the same access.

Similarly, Scotland has committed to increasing early years education provision, but a focused understanding of the needs of children and young people with additional support needs will be needed if equality is to be assured for Scotland's disabled children. Our experience in The Yard demonstrates that Scotland still falls short of its goal of supporting *all* disabled children and their families. We should not be getting it right for *most* children in Scotland but for *every* child in Scotland. □

20. People and places – from Mapira to Govan

Jamie Livingstone, Oxfam Scotland

There is inequality in Scotland but also worldwide: we should tackle it wherever it exists.

WORKING for an organisation with a vision to end poverty and suffering everywhere creates countless impossible choices every day. I switch focus multiple times between tackling poverty in Scotland and in 'less developed' countries. If I stop to think about the implicit prioritisation that requires, I feel deeply uncomfortable.

I get a similar feeling when I ask someone to donate money to help people in one of the world's many humanitarian crises only to be told 'sorry, charity begins at home'. To me, that approach puts one person's suffering above another's based on where they live, not the depth of their need. It's an approach I choose not to adopt.

Instead, I want to tell you about two very different, but equally inspirational, places: one in Scotland and one 7,000 miles away in Malawi. I also want to explain why I invest hope in the Sustainable Development Goals (SDGs) as a vehicle for building global solidarity and outline some of the core elements of a more human economy.

In late 2016 I travelled to Malawi amid a food crisis that left 6.5 million people hungry. I met Jenipher, a small-holder farmer looking after three orphaned nephews. Her crop was destroyed by drought and she had no idea where her family's next meal was coming from. Her eyes revealed the depth of her despair; it was palpable. Later, as a local government officer explained the emergency response, I spotted a copy of the SDGs pinned to the wall behind him. It hammered home the global nature of the Goals and the fact their success or failure rests far from the corridors of the United Nations.

I then visited Mapira, a village around 30 minutes' drive from Malawi's capital, Lilongwe. I watched as the farmers hand-bucketed water upstream to ensure their new solar-powered irrigation pumps wouldn't run dry. As well as helping them adapt to climate change, Oxfam is supporting the villagers to pursue their own vision for the future.

Chalked on a wall in the village were their very own 'Sustainable Development Goals': improved food security; access to safe water; and better homes, complete with corrug-ated iron roofs. The villagers had agreed what needed to happen to achieve each goal, what they could do, what help they needed and, crucially, who would do what and by when. There were small but tangible signs of progress: from their new income generating barber shop, tucked away inside a small thatched shack, to the village shop next door selling basic essentials brought from the city. I felt an enviable unity of purpose and overwhelming solidarity: the villagers' fate was so deeply intertwined.

It reminded me of the feeling I get when I visit GalGael, an organisation in the heart of Govan in Glasgow; their sawdust strewn workshop is a place I have been drawn back to again and again. GalGael doesn't see itself as a charity with a mission to 'fix' those who walk through its doors. Instead, it is a community of creative people who come together to make wooden items, like furniture, and to cooperatively meet some of the community's needs.

Participants – many of whom face complex challenges ranging from poverty to addiction, mental health issues and more besides – are offered a workbench, tools and respect as the basis of their individual journeys. The organisation's commitment to solidarity and equality is made physical during weekly assemblies where decisions are collectively discussed and agreed. They are sawing and chiselling their way forward, together.

In doing so, the people of Govan – like those in Mapira – are showing huge leadership, but the challenges they are battling have their roots in a broken economic model that concentrates wealth in the hands of a tiny elite. Globally, just eight people own the same wealth as the 3.6 billion who make up the poorest half of humanity. All eight of these individuals are men. Far from trickling down, income and wealth are being sucked upwards. That may be forgivable if one in nine people weren't surviving on less than $2 a day. Progress is being made, but not fast enough.

Encouragingly, there is increasing recognition of the fact that extreme economic inequality is undermining the fight against poverty. In agreeing the SDGs, world leaders committed to both ending extreme poverty by 2030 and 'leaving no-one behind'. Yet these SDGs are linked: ending extreme poverty won't be achieved without reducing inequality and it is clear that policy tweaks will not be enough.

Frustratingly, the measures needed to narrow the gap – at home and abroad – are well known. National governments must recognise that while markets can be a vital engine for growth and prosperity, they should no longer steer the car. They need careful management to ensure the proceeds are shared fairly. That means ensuring economies work for women as well as men; tackling in-work poverty; limiting executive pay; and encouraging business models that do not give undue reward to shareholders. It also means using progressive taxation to fund social protection as well as decent healthcare and education.

Yet the political will to implement such measures is too often lacking, or inadequate. The uncomfortable question is – why? One answer is that wealth is often used to entrench inequality not reduce it. Not only can wealthier people live longer, healthier lives, but their money also buys them power. Laws and policies are often bent to reinforce their position; the global network of tax havens is perhaps the clearest example.

Public anger is bubbling, and inequality has been cited as a factor in the election of Donald Trump, as well as President Duerte in the Philippines and Brexit. Such political shockwaves could just be the beginning. As President Obama said in 2016: 'A world where 1 per cent of humanity controls as much wealth as the bottom 99 per cent will never be stable'. Yet, as Nobel Prize-winning economist Professor Joseph Stiglitz has made clear, extreme economic inequality 'is something that we create, by our policies, by what we do'. It is long past time for us to collectively press the 'undo' button.

In doing so, we must recognise that change at national level, whether in Malawi or closer to home, will be critical. Here in Scotland, income inequality has remained broadly stable since rising sharply in the 1980s, but the incomes of the highest earning 1-2 per cent have pulled away. Wealth – property, assets like savings and shares, as well as pensions – is even more unequally shared with the richest 1 per cent owning more than the bottom 50 per cent put together.

A large majority of people in Scotland say they want to live in a more equal country. Yet, if talking about fairness actually delivered it, Scotland would already be a beacon of equality. We have seen no shortage of welcome initiatives by the Scottish Government to make Scotland fairer but, while politicians here are more awake and aware of these issues both they, and perhaps those who elect them, are still hiding under the covers. Significant levers to reduce inequality remain at UK-level, but the Scottish Parliament has a growing array of powers it could now use and the case for doing so is clear.

Nearly one in five people in Scotland live in relative poverty and hundreds of thousands of food parcels are handed out by emergency food providers each year. That's children, women and men in rich Scotland going hungry; extreme food insecurity co-existing with extreme wealth. Some question the validity of comparing relative poverty in Scotland – measured as those earning less than 60 per cent of the median household income – and extreme poverty overseas. Yet everyone should have the ability not just to survive, but to participate fully in society. Put bluntly, should I care more that Jenipher and her nephews are going hungry in Malawi or that a single mum and her kids are forced to turn to a foodbank in Scotland? It's a choice I'm unwilling to make.

The transition to a more human economy – whether in Mapira or Govan – will be far from quick but we must be impatient for change for everyone in poverty. Communities are leading the way, and now our politics – with the SDGs as a roadmap – must catch up.   □

21. Shared spaces

Diarmaid Lawlor, Architecture and Design Scotland

The physical spaces we live in – our buildings, streets
and public places – affect the quality of our relationships
with each other. We need places that allow us to live
together in supportive relationships, to share our lives,
not to isolate us from each other.

MY neighbour has dementia. Sometimes, my children and I call
round. As a child, she performed in theatres. Today, she sings
to stay in touch with the world she once knew. My children
listen. They join in. The space of the song connects them. It
becomes an emotional geography, a shared place between
generations, across wellness and infirmity. It is a space where
each participant can just be.

I wonder, in our places, where are our day-to-day spaces to
connect? And, how do we create these places in every
community, so there is equity of provision and equality in terms
of outcome, regardless of socio-economic class?

I once tried to think about how neighbourhoods change. I
think there are four ways this happens. First, there is the crisis.
Something has to be done, and fast. Solutions happen. The
second is the place on the edge: things looks ok, but behind
the scenes they aren't great. The strategy is the sticking plaster.
The third is the place where investment is planned such as a
new school, or some housing. People begin to think about
stretching the possibilities. I call the fourth 'comfortably numb'

– things aren't great but it's hard to mobilise any interest for change. A common feature in each kind of place is the need and desire for people to connect, but the lack of opportunities to do so.

Look around neighbourhoods and you'll see spaces which have been designed for one use only, or are managed by one interest group only. These are the scout halls and church halls and school halls, and empty shops, and half-used parks and bowling clubs managed by members, and community groups operating out of worn-out buildings for cheap rent. Sometimes in some places the spaces are there, but still there is loneliness, isolation, lack of agency, resilience, participation and positive destinations. Why?

The modern generation can get information on any issue anywhere on the internet. What they really need, they say, are spaces to make sense of things. Educationalists say that experience is not learning. Learning is about reflecting on experience. Reflection is about building the conditions for safe and honest sharing, and sense making. Imagine if we designed all neighbourhoods as lifelong learning places, shared spaces to make sense. To do that, our model of making places work would not be about single investments for single uses for single groups some of the time. The model would be about building more opportunities for more people to connect more through sharing spaces. It would also be about protecting some spaces to just be. To be quiet, and away from things.

The community of Coigach recently built a boat. This is a remote community in the West Highlands, where the place itself is a strong emotional shared connection between families. As part of this project, people came together to plan making the boat by the half light in a shed near the sea. Men, women and young people shared tasks. Some were good at carpentry, some learning. The focus was the boat. This is the connecting space. It connects men who may not have worked together, the sexes, generations. The consequence of building the boat is a stronger more connected community.

I like this story because it has a strong central focus that is tangible. It invites participation on a number of scales. People can plan, paint, launch, celebrate, lift, problem solve around something that those in that place understand and participate in. The focus fits the place. Spaces to connect might be projects, hosted in spaces we already have, adapted to enable multiple connections and possibilities.

The regeneration of Pennywell in Edinburgh, one of the most deprived areas in the city, seeks to transform the life of the community. A delegation from the community visited Mannheim in Germany to explore ideas about co-producing regeneration. The focus was to explore what happens when the community is a partner in shaping the actions and outcomes of the regeneration process using different forms of citizen participation. In Mannheim, 'tree adopters' tend to the street trees outside their houses to enhance the sense of place. As they garden, people stop to talk. At the level of small groups, shared gardens are enabling an emergent form of community around growing and celebrating the land. At the formal community level, spaces for conversation and innovation, and non- hierarchical spaces have been developed as part of the governance system. These spaces invite the community to share the process of shaping the city. Participation in making places better is about different kinds of shared space to enable different citizens to find their place in the community. It isn't all about agendas and meetings. And the principle of finding the right kinds of space for the community to participate is the same for rural and urban communities. The spaces look different. The principles are the same.

One of the places the community from Pennywell visited was Vauban in the city of Freiburg. This community developed from environmental activism in the 1970s and 80s into a sustainable neighbourhood, with energy efficient architecture and communal governance. It is a fantastic place for families but the children have become teenagers and young adults have aged. The place, designed for families, doesn't have spaces to make it a great place to grow old or be a teenager. And the values that created that place are not necessarily the values shared by the new generation. Places change and we constantly need the spaces to accommodate these changes. In all communities we also need conversations on the values, norms and identities that changing places require. Investing in shared spaces based on a principle of equity of provision and equality of outcome for all communities in all places would be a great way to foster this culture of adaptability.

The most profound learning is that which happens when we listen. Stories, like songs, carry knowledge from generation to generation. They contain tacit knowledge, understood by communities. They are spaces that can invite participation, spaces that can be shared, and practised. The shared spaces of the built environment can support and share new knowledge, empathy and opportunity.   □

22. Small steps, slow journeys

Caroline Gibb, Equality and Rights Network

How do we begin to make a real difference to people's lives? By starting small, and working together.

WORKING in the voluntary sector, particularly for small community projects that are low on resources and have finite funding, can be testing. While feeling consistently limited by time, energy and money and a narrow focus on targets and outcomes, it's easy to wonder what difference we can possibly make. How can we realise our aims to tackle poverty and inequality? Where do you even start?

You start by listening to people. You facilitate. You get creative. You aim big, and you start small. By adopting a community development approach you allow people to recognise and develop their own ability and potential. You help groups organise themselves to respond to shared problems and needs.

Building on this can help to create strong communities, communities that work together to promote social justice and help improve the quality of community life. It can also enable those communities to work together with public agencies to improve the quality of government. But to start building, you need foundations.

I can share many, many inspiring stories from years of working for under-resourced community projects in areas with high levels of poverty, inequality and isolation. They are all stories of starting small. Here are three of them.

Susie was a young mother who was referred to adult community cooking classes. She came along to the first of ten sessions with a key worker and was terrified. The session leaders didn't know her background and didn't ask her any questions. She was pale and shaking, couldn't make eye contact and could hardly speak. She struggled to leave her baby in the crèche. She repeatedly said that she couldn't cook.

By week five, Susie told the session leaders that she and her sister-in-law had decided to start a 'Come Dine with Me' challenge every weekend, and that she was using the recipes she was given in the sessions. She kept the session leaders up to date on this, and then started asking for advice on other techniques and recipes that they hadn't covered.

By the end of the ten weeks, Susie was like a different person. She was chatty and confident and had made friends with other people in the group. She told the session leaders she and her family were eating better and that the cooking sessions were life changing.

Louise was a single mother of two young children who began volunteering in a fruit and vegetable co-op a couple of days a week. She struggled with depression, was living in poverty and refused to take what she called 'handouts'. Volunteering was a way for her to fight against this, to feel useful. Louise came and went, but even when not volunteering she would be in touch. She would pop in and chat and keep the staff up to date. She talked often of her kids and their achievements. She managed to get paid work as a cleaner, something she was very proud of.

However, what she really enjoyed was the volunteering work she had done, working in and with the community. She talked a lot about this, and then one of the staff suggested she go on a community development course. Louise laughed – she wasn't cut out for that! But she went away and thought about it. Maybe she was?

She did go on that course and she loved it. She went on to do a college course, and then found out that she had been accepted on to a university degree course in community development. Her children, by then in high school, helped her fill out the application and would leave her notes saying 'You're doing awesome, mum.' Louise began proudly taking all the handouts she is entitled to.

Mary was in her 60s, recently retired from a job she had done for almost 40 years. Living alone, she was feeling a bit lost now she was no longer working. When she was doing her shopping one day she saw a sign about a walking group. She didn't ask about it right away. But eventually she found out that it ran every Friday, was for all ages, and everyone stopped for a cup of tea and a chat afterwards. One Friday she turned up for the walk, and then came back every Friday after that. She got to know the other women in the group and soon began to take newer members under her wing. Some of these people were not those she would ever have met or spoken to before. She became particularly friendly with Sheila, another older woman who lived alone. Sheila had been very isolated and struggled with social situations and for a while wouldn't join group activities. But she had been going to the walking group for a while and she and Mary hit it off. After a while, they began meeting each other every Tuesday to go for a walk together.

These stories are not just about cooking, or volunteering, or walking. They are about loneliness, isolation, poverty and marginalisation. They are about using a community development approach to create opportunities for change, about people taking control of their lives. They are about small steps and slow journeys. This could be done through food, volunteering, walking; or through art, music or sport.

Karen is a young disabled woman who volunteers as an Equalities Ambassador with the Equality and Rights Network. She does this because she feels strongly that 'people who are facing barriers for whatever reason, whether it is because of age, gender, disability, sexuality etcetera, should be the ones who have the voice to change things. We have the lived experience so we know what can make things fairer.'

Community development is about allowing room for people to find and use their own voices. It is also about finding ways for those voices to be heard. It's about working together to create meaningful change.   ☐

Reflections

Danny Murphy, Richard Freeman and Fiona McHardy

THE multiple perspectives offered in the different chapters of this book shine a light on only some of the many issues of equality and inequality in contemporary Scotland. The multi-layered, kaleidoscopic character of these issues, extending from the level of the individual to the international, and across different aspects of our individual and social identities, is one of the reasons that it is difficult to grasp the full nature of inequality. It also makes it difficult to define what would constitute an acceptable equality. This then makes it important to understand both the strengths and the limitations of these concepts of equality and inequality: to realise that there are many possible more equal futures, not just one, and to imagine what some of them might be. Without such understanding, it will be hard to recognise the different types of actions that may help take us forward.

Developing this understanding is a task not just for politicians, policy makers and practitioners. If we are to build a more equal Scotland, every individual, every part of the civic community, will need to be involved. It may require a reconfiguration of how we understand and practise social solidarity. Some of the traditional foundations of this have been eroded in recent decades as they have come under intellectual attack from neo-liberal individualism and economic pressure from the fragment-ation of employment patterns.

Taking action is important, but so too is using the right

language. Leaping into action can be counterproductive if there is no clear understanding of what is at stake – if meanings are not shared, if the language we use does not accurately describe the problem. We need a language that can capture the insights shared in this book, a language that can give our discussions a firm foundation. Equality and inequality are general concepts which capture important aspects of social experience but they are so broad in scope that they can conceal as much as they reveal. The ideas with which we frame the discussion and organise our thinking can open up or close down our exploration of equality. Before we can take action, we need to ask what we mean by equality.

There are different kinds of equalities – income and wealth, clearly, but also input and outcome, value, opportunity, experience, respect, and physical and mental health among many other things. Equality is not just about the distribution of resources, but also about relationships. One way of capturing this is to make use of the older democratic concept of 'fraternity' which, stripped of its gendered overtones, brings warmth, concern, empathy and care to what might otherwise be merely transactional relationships. We do not seek an equality of impersonal sameness, but an equality of agency, an equality of respect, an equality of value, an equality that recognises and values difference. This kind of equality can work with the potentially conflicting foundational democratic value of liberty: liberty, with its emphasis on freedoms, rights and choices, can damage equality if taken to extreme. Using appeals to liberty, individuals or groups can use their advantages of power and wealth to advance their own interests at the expense of others, or of the community as a whole. Finding the right balance between liberty and equality is a task for democratic community, and key to it is the related value of equity – fairness. Again and again in our discussions, it was an equality not of sameness that was sought, but of fairness.

Equality matters. It matters for utilitarian reasons, because more equal societies experience social and economic benefits such as improved well-being, improved health and improved economic performance, among others. But it matters for moral reasons, too: it's just plain wrong that some members of our society, of our local and global as well as national communities, are scarred by their experience of poverty – poverty in income and opportunities and the poverty of not being valued equally, of not being granted the equal dignity to which all of us are entitled as of right.

National and local governments have many levers they can pull to address inequalities, and their role is essential. They provide direction and a framework. They set the terms of discussion. Government can contribute either to greater equality or to greater inequality – by planning and target setting, legislating and regulating, raising and distributing revenue, auditing and accounting – in many parts of our public life. But the power and importance of the role of government may sometimes lead to problems being framed solely in political terms and politics being seen as the only source of solutions. The 'top down' actions of government are essential, but they are unlikely ever to be enough to eliminate inequality.

For policies need to be mediated locally and individually. Some of the most effective actions in tackling inequalities are local, relational, face-to-face. They may be quite independent of government and its formal channels: in democratic communities, power flows in many different directions. Third sector organisations make a difference, and local partnerships bring people and organisations together. Individuals and households exert power in the everyday social and economic choices they make. Every level of action is important in the politics of equality.

Speaking and listening are important actions, too. Listening to and engaging with different voices and the different experiences of equality and inequality can improve policy responses. But this is not the only reason to listen, to respect the voices and stories of others. The generalities we search for in statistics are hugely significant, but the stories and the people behind them are important, too. Having your voice heard, being listened to, is in some way to become more equal, independently of any other aspect of equality or inequality.

Processes such as community participatory research can give voice to those whose lived experience is not heard equally in national policy or public media. In hearing these different voices, listening to these stories, we appreciate that equality and inequality are many faceted and that the top-down solutions of national government need to be embodied various different ways: In the face-to-face relationships of individuals, in the realities of our lives in our communities of work and leisure, and in our homes and our hearts. This book testifies to the many levels at which responses to inequality can make a difference.

Diverse responses are important in their own right, but also enhance each other through communication and interaction. One of the benefits of the work in our group was to listen to the work and experience of others, to realise the kaleidoscopic nature of inequalities of contemporary life and the many ways in which equality can be promoted and delivered.

Whatever is achieved by policy, equality must be realised and made effective by the commitments of practitioners, both professional and voluntary. It will also be realised by our interaction with each other as political citizens and economic actors engaged in processes of production, consumption and exchange. But much can be achieved through the actions of individual human beings, each of whom is of equal value. It is not just in the actions of government that unfair inequalities will be tackled but in the lives of individual citizens, in our relationships and our actions, in the shared spaces of the public realm where we meet with each other face-to-face. □

Other books in the series

1. AfterNow – What next for a healthy Scotland?
| *Phil Hanlon/Sandra Carlisle*
The authors of this visionary book look at health in Scotland
and beyond health to the main social, economic,
environmental and cultural challenges of our times. They
examine the type of transformational change required to
create a more resilient and healthy Scotland.

2. The Great Takeover – How materialism, the media
and markets now dominate our lives | *Carol Craig*
Describes the dominance of materalist values, the media
and business in all our lives and how this is leading to a loss
of individual and collective well-being. It looks at many of
the big issues of our times – debt, inequality, political apathy,
loss of self-esteem, pornography and the rise of celebrity
culture. The conclusion is simple and ultimately hopeful – we
can change our values and our lives.

3. The New Road – Charting Scotland's inspirational
communities | *Alf Young / Ewan Young*
A father and son go on a week long journey round Scotland
to see at first hand some of the great environmental, social,
employment and regeneration projects which are
happening. From Dunbar in the south east of Scotland to
Knoydart in the north west they meet people involved in
projects which demonstrate new ways of living.

4. Scotland's Local Food Revolution | *Mike Small*
Lifts the lid on the unsavoury reality of our current food system including horsemeat in processed beef products, the unsustainable movement of food round the globe, and how supermarket shopping generates massive waste. It's an indictment of a food syste that is out of control. But there is hope – the growth and strength of Scotland's local food movement.

5. Letting Go – Breathing new life into organisations | *Tony Miller/ Gordon Hall*
It is now commonplace for employees to feel frustrated at work – ground down by systems that are dominated by rules, protocols, guidelines, targets and inspections. Tony Miller and Gordon Hall explore the origins of 'command and control' management as well as the tyranny of modern day 'performance management'. Effective leaders, they argue, should 'let go' of their ideas on controlling staff and nurture intrinsic motivation instead.

6. Raising Spirits – Allotments, well-being and community | *Jenny Mollison/ Judy Wilkinson/ Rona Wilkinson*
Allotments are the unsung story of our times; hidden places for food, friendship and freedom from the conformity of everyday life. A fascinating look at how allotments came about; why they can make such a substantial contribution to health, well-being, community, food production, and the environment; and what's happening in other countries.

7. Schooling Scotland – Education, equity and community | *Daniel Murphy*
The Scottish schooling system does well for many children growing up in Scotland, but to ensure that all children get the education they deserve, a better partnership of parent, child, school, government and society is needed – one to which all Scotland can contribute and from which all children can benefit. Daniel Murphy suggests eight ways to ensure that Scottish education could be stronger and fairer.

8. Shaping our Global Future – A guide for young people | *Derek Brown*
Young people worry about the future world they will live in: personal futures, families and jobs. But they also worry about their global futures. The possibilities and challenges ahead appear overwhelming. This guide to human achievements and future challenges is designed to help young people consider the future their children and grandchildren will inhabit.

9. Conviction – Violence, culture and a shared public service agenda | *John Carnochan* Policeman John Carnochan takes us on a memorable journey of discovery as he comes to grips with violence and Scotland's traditionally high murder rate. He also gives a fascinating insight into the work of Scotland's Violence Reduction Unit and why it has been so spectacularly successful. This compelling book is not about high visibility policing or more officers but the importance of empathy and children's early years.

10. She, He, They – Families, gender and coping with transition | *Shirley Young*
How challenging can gender transition be for both parents and siblings? A story of hope and resilience, it shows that if parents can move beyond the shock and pain of their offspring's transition, all family members can come closer together and experience life-enhancing change.

11. Knowing and Growing – Insights for developing ourselves and others | *Alan McLean*
This extraordinary book provides insights and practical tools to help you navigate everyday human interactions, balance your own and others' needs and utilise your emotions to create a more fulfilling life. The powerful insights readers glean from 'McLean's Ring' are not only helpful for parents, teachers and leaders they are also essential for anyone aiming to encourage others to grow and develop as individuals.

More titles are planned for 2017 and 2018.
Books can be ordered from
www.postcardsfromscotland.co.uk or from
www.amazon.co.uk Kindle editions are also available.